Shopping Behavior in Asia

# Shopping Behavior
# in Asia

## What Retailers Need to Know
## for Success in the Far East

## Laurent Sausset

PMP
Paramount Market Publishing, Inc.

Paramount Market Publishing, Inc.
950 Danby Road, Suite 136
Ithaca, NY 14850
www.paramountbooks.com
Voice: 607-275-8100; 888-787-8100
Fax: 607-275-8101

Publisher: James Madden
Editorial Director: Doris Walsh

Cataloging in Publication Data available
ISBN 13: 978-0-9830436-5-2 | ISBN 10: 0-9830436-5-5

To my father, Michel, and
to my wife Siriwan, with love

# Contents

# Acknowledgments

FIRST AND FOREMOST, I would like to sincerely thank the dozens of clients who over the years trusted me and shared the marketing challenges their retail chains have been facing in Asia. I am indebted to the top management for their confidence but also to the hundreds of thousands of shoppers in the Far East for the answers they provided, either to quantitative questionnaires or during focus groups. Without their input and their patience, this book could not have been written.

Among the research partners we worked with in Asia, I received help and cooperation in particular from Tommy Leung, Hiroshi Aoyama, Dea-Jun Koh, Carol Cheong, Pimwalunch Sarachai, Rawisuda Senawatin and Achmad Noorsubchan. My gratitude also goes to the project managers with DistriSurvey Ltd, for their professional and dedicated work, as well as to friends for their invaluable observations. My thanks go to Grit Wangwattana, Joe Lin, Miyuki Yamabe, Betty Kao, Calvin Wang, Suksun Muenprasitivej, Santos Thenu, Low Wai Min, Thanapon Tangkananan and to my wife Siriwan for her love and unique way to understand and point out behaviors of Asian people. I am also particularly grateful to my editor Doris Walsh, for her comments and help which provided more rhythm to this work, and to her team for their assistance and efficient copyediting.

As I acknowledge the support and cooperation that I received from so many persons, I wish to emphasize that I am solely responsible for the content of this book and for any imprecision it may contain.

# Introduction

A FEW YEARS AGO, at a meeting with an Asian Director with an international retail banner, I was told something that went more or less like this: "You know, our customers in Asia, what they want at the end of the day, it's nice price, a large assortment, and a good service. That's the key."

This declaration sounds good. However, the problem is that it is doesn't say anything at all. In what way is a price a nice price? What is a large assortment? And how do you define good service?

In this book we'll try to go a little deeper than a textbook statement and aim to review the customers' needs and wants in Asia. What do they look for in relation to price? Is it the same with promotions? Is there a difference between the price image of a store and its promotion image? Is there a difference whether the business is a food retailer, such as a supermarket or a hypermarket, or whether it's a category killer, like a DIY specialist or a fashion retailer? Other than price, what can we say about product range in the Far East for all those store formats? How do Asian shoppers experience service in terms of facilities such as parking lot, store signage, or cleanliness and in interaction with employees?

When relevant we will compare with shoppers in the West but this book is primarily about the shopping behavior of Asian people. It is based on surveys in northeast Asia (Korea and Japan), Greater China (Hong Kong, Taiwan, the People's Republic of China) and most of the Southeast Asian nations (Thailand, Malaysia, Singapore, Indonesia, Vietnam,

Cambodia, Laos). In these markets, whenever there are some ethnic or religious minorities that appear significant, their shopping behavior will be addressed as well.

We will illustrate that some attitudes and behaviors are similar in all these Far East countries. People like to believe they are unique or special but in Asia, some cultural traits are comparable whether you are in northeast or Southeast Asia and whether you are a Shanghainese in China or a Ho Chi Minh City resident in Vietnam. Other than culture, we will also emphasize two determinants that impact shopping: demographics and physical conditions in the first two chapters..

We will then visit a typical store in Asia and indicate what we think retailers need to do *before* they open a store, at the expansion stage, and *after*, in terms of operations and commercial offer. We'll aim to pinpoint the parameters that really count for a store to be successful in the Far East markets. To conclude, we'll examine how retail might evolve in Asia in the next few decades.

# 1

# Market Commonalities and Differences

THE JAPANESE commonly say, "We are unique." For many Japanese, even the snow in their country is different. Koreans will allege, "Our country is different from the rest of the world." In China, people will explain that the mainland is very diverse and you cannot even compare the north like Beijing, with southern cities like Guangzhou, "It's like various separate countries." If a Taiwanese businessman talks about consumers with a partner residing in the PRC, they will feel that China is a different market from Taiwan, yet both are Chinese and they are talking about Chinese consumers. In Malaysia people will tell you, "We have two large communities, Malays and Chinese living together and because of that, our country is unlike any other." In Thailand, "Because we are Buddhists, we have a very specific perspective about life."

All this is true up to a point, but the same kind of assumption exists everywhere; all countries can be considered different from one another. However, common traits can also be found throughout Asia. If you spend several days in the Far East, or even several years, you may have the impression that Asian countries have simply become Westernized. You might think that traditional Asia is basically giving way to modern lifestyles. After all, in Tokyo or Kuala Lumpur people go to work every morning and come back home every evening as in the West; they commute with cars, air-conditioned buses, or modern subways, and you may feel those public transports are similar, and actually safer and cleaner perhaps, than in most Western cities.

If you are in a car in a large city of China, you will experience as many traffic jams as anywhere in the West. In 2011, there were nearly 5 million cars in Beijing, more than in Los Angeles. Potentially you will hear more car horns in Shanghai or Beijing than you would in Paris or New York as Chinese drivers express their impatience. If you decide to walk around in Shanghai, you'll feel surrounded by prominent skyscrapers. In Jakarta you may see a twin-building residence that's the tallest in the world. In South Korea, you cannot fail to notice the thousands of apartment buildings in Seoul or Pusan where two-thirds of the population resides, not unlike in big cities in Europe. You may also feel that half of the city dwellers in Asia own PDAs or smartphones. Indeed, it is estimated that for the year 2011 there were 177 million smartphone users in Asia Pacific (including Australia and New Zealand) versus 97 million in Western Europe and 104 million for the USA.

Some Asian markets like Korea, Hong Kong, Singapore, and Japan are already developed but even in emerging countries, everyone aspires to be modernized, which to them means to live and consume like in the West. Therefore, you may feel that the cultural heritage is rapidly being forgotten and the social structure has profoundly changed. It appears as if middle classes already exist everywhere in Asia or are emerging rapidly, and it looks like all these people are simply heading towards a Westernized way of life.

In terms of shopping too, you may feel that daily life in Asia has become similar with the West. In Japan, you are likely to see as many convenience stores like 7-Eleven as you would in the United States. In China, millions of Chinese people do their shopping at international chains like Walmart, Tesco, or Carrefour every week and they buy yogurt and TV dinners, which are not traditional foods. All the major international retailers appear to be present in Asia.

In fact, the Far East in the current decade is perhaps situated at a pivotal moment of its history, as the region is transforming into a Westernized world but at the same time, it is also retaining its core culture. Granted,

Asian people go to their workplace by subway, and office hours are roughly the same as in the West, but an Asian blue-collar worker does not have the same way of thinking nor the same cultural background as a westerner. Relationships at work and family links are still very traditional and quite homogeneous in all Asian countries. For instance, family bonds are not focused on the relationship between parents and young children; they are somewhat broader.

One can illustrate these points with examples about daily life such as a white-collar worker who wants to take a week's vacation or a family whose son is studying away from home.

In the West, an employee who wants a week's vacation would ask his boss for the time and at some point probably would casually tell his colleagues that he's planning to remodel part of his home or needs to spend a week with the children. If he is entitled to it, and if the company workload is not too heavy at the time, he will get his vacation week and he'll spend it at home if that's his plan.

If the Asian white-collar worker has vacation days accrued and if the company is not at peak season, he can get a week off as well. However, he will not say casually that he plans some do-it-yourself projects at home. On the contrary, he will clearly and officially tell his boss, in particular, that he'll be 500 kilometers away, visiting his old uncle and that if necessary, he can be reached via cellphone only. If he doesn't say this, he suspects that two things may happen. Perhaps his boss will comment that one week at home seems too much and if there's no travel involved, a couple of days off should suffice. The boss cannot dictate his vacation place nor impose a duration of only two days of course, but he can certainly comment in this way. For the employee, it would be embarrassing. So an application for a leave or some personal time, if it's to be one week long, is likely to be carefully phrased. The other possibility an Asian employee envisions is that on his first or second day off if he's at home, he might receive a phone call from his chief, for an urgent matter. The boss would call and ask him to come back at the office, just for a couple of hours, no more, for a task that he can tackle better than his colleagues.

The boss is not a bad person trying to ruin his annual leave; he is just thinking that work is a priority and it's normal to interrupt a vacation. The Asian employee cannot answer, "Sorry boss, I can't come; I'm in the middle of re-painting my kitchen," because in some way it would damage respect towards his superior. So he will respond something like, "Sure, I'll be at the office in an hour." None of this can happen if he is 500 kilometers away at the other end of the country though; that's why he is officially visiting his old uncle.

Another example of cultural differences between Asians and Westerners could relate to parents and their young-adult children. In a Western country, suppose a son in his mid-twenties, who studies at a university far away from home, comes back on a Saturday afternoon, unannounced, to visit his parents. His parents happen to have visitors when he arrives. Basically the parents are very happy to see their son and everybody has a good time; it is simple and casual.

In Asia, the situation will appear to be almost exactly the same, but again with a slight difference. The Asian parents, also having visitors (the neighbors or some relatives, for instance) are very happy to see their son come back home for a couple of days and everybody will have a good time, too. So, where is the difference? The Asian parents are not simply happy to see their son, they are also very proud because they gained face towards the neighbors who were visiting. Nothing was proclaimed, but the whole scene was saying to the visitors, "You see how our family is close and united. Our son lives so far away but he cares about us and comes to see his old parents." This non-verbal message is actually as important as the visit itself. The parents are genuinely happy to receive their son, of course, but in addition, it is good in terms of their image towards the visitors. Face is social; it's about what others will think of you and how they will see you, whether you are a white-collar worker or the proud mother of a university student. It is part of the culture in all Asian countries.

## Traditional shopping behaviors

So even though the Far East is modernizing, you can still notice behaviors that are traditional. It is the case for shopping too. People do shop at wet markets for fresh produce or traditional markets for furniture in Asia, in both emerging countries and in advanced economies. In Japan you still see young ladies wearing kimonos in subways or in department stores. In the streets of Bangkok, which is modernizing quickly, you may even encounter an elephant or two from time to time near stores or markets.

In most Asian countries, people still go to temples to ask for blessings and they will consult fortunetellers even when they are highly educated. When a supermarket or any modern trade store opens, feng shui specialists, monks, or other masters depending on the country, will conduct ceremonies to bring protection and blessing to the new store. Events such as Lunar New Year and traditional festivals are still present in family life and impact the consumption because people will buy specific foods and gifts. In a given year, these traditional events can represent more than one third of the annual sales turnover for some producers of upscale foods and beverages in Asia. For instance, around August each year, the Ghost Festival in Chinese markets is a spiritual celebration but it is also a commercial event involving shows, opera, or concerts as well as buying and offering foods, dinners and expensive liquors. Similar annual events take place in Japan (Ochugen in July or in August), Korea (Chuseok in September) and Vietnam (Wandering Souls Day in August) where people buy meat, fruit and rice cakes or deliver gifts to relatives or business acquaintances.

While several interconnections evolve, between local traditions and western life, cultural traits still exist in Asia and they reflect quite homogeneous behaviors and attitudes. These interconnections have an impact on the consumption habits of today everywhere in the Far East. This book about Asian shoppers is also about this interaction between traditional ways of thinking and the behavior linked with shopping either at wet markets or at modern trade (modern trade here means that prices are fixed and not negotiable). Before addressing what the Asian cultures have in common however, there are two determinants that affect shopping and need to be pointed out.

## Demographics

What exactly would cause people to buy one product or another? One determinant is what we call demographics—characteristics like age, gender, level of education, or income. Let's consider age groups. Compare three emerging markets, China, the Philippines and Indonesia. Indonesia has approximately 27 to 28 percent of people who are aged 14 and under. About 35 percent fall into this category in the Philippines whereas China has a much lower ratio of these young people, only 18 percent. Then, if we look at the average age of a hypermarket shopper in Jakarta it is age 31 or 32, but late thirties in Shanghai. Whether shoppers are in their early thirties or ten years older, it makes a difference if you think of what people will buy for food, clothing, or for the home.

Population by Country 2011, in millions

| | Total Population | Population by Age (in % of total) | | |
|---|---|---|---|---|
| | | 0–14 years | 15–64 years | 65+ years |
| Cambodia | 14.7 | 32.2% | 64.1% | 3.8% |
| China | 1,335.7 | 17.6 | 73.6 | 8.9 |
| Hong Kong | 7.1 | 11.6 | 74.8 | 13.5 |
| Indonesia | 245.6 | 27.3 | 66.5 | 6.1 |
| Japan | 126.5 | 13.1 | 64.0 | 22.9 |
| Malaysia | 28.7 | 29.6 | 65.4 | 3.8 |
| Philippines | 101.8 | 34.6 | 61.1 | 4.3 |
| Singapore | 4.7 | 13.8 | 77.0 | 9.2 |
| South Korea | 48.8 | 15.7 | 72.9 | 11.4 |
| Taiwan | 23.1 | 15.6 | 73.4 | 10.9 |
| Thailand | 66.7 | 19.9 | 70.9 | 9.2 |
| Vietnam | 90.5 | 25.2 | 69.3 | 5.5 |

*Source: U.S. Central Intelligence Agency*

Family structure is another determinant. In the parts of China where households have one child, there is an obvious impact on the demand for children's apparel and toys. Parents will tend to buy very nice products for their kid (also known as "little emperor") but since there is only one child they will purchase a limited number of toys. In the case of Indonesia or the Philippines, if a family has the same income as the Chinese household but they have four children, purchase of toys and clothing will not be the same. The Indonesian or Filipino parents will purchase more toys in total, but perhaps with a lower ticket value for each.

Income also has an impact on spending that is quite easy to understand. If a family earns the equivalent of USD 10,000 per year and another earns USD 30,000 per year, the shopping behaviors will be different; the shoppers will buy different things, at different price points, even if they are the same age, the same gender and belong to the same ethnic background. For instance, in China you will be able to buy a car if you reach a certain personal income, which is around USD 600 per month. Below this threshold you will not be able to own a car and beyond it, you will. Based on the successive income thresholds, you may reach the purchasing power to own a luxury car. The selection of a specific brand is a separate issue; it will depend upon several variables that include personal shopping criteria and the positioning of the brands. But, from a macroeconomic point of view, demographics will play a major part in shopping behavior in terms of categories of products purchased.

Before we talk about another important driver, physical conditions, let's review a key point about demographics, which is how much money households have at their disposal in Asia.

## A few details about income and households

Standards of living vary widely among Asian markets but for simplicity, we can distinguish two groups. First are the developed markets like Japan, Korea, Hong Kong, Taiwan, and Singapore, where, according to the IMF World Economic Outlook issued in April 2011, the GDP per capita is projected for year 2012 to range between around USD 25,000 and 45,000 (or even more in case of Japan and Singapore). These income levels are not so different than in countries like Italy, France, or Germany (USD 36,000–45,000), especially since the IMF numbers show a 6 or 7 percent yearly growth trend between 2008 and 2012 in countries like South Korea or Taiwan and no growth (a slight decline actually) in France, Italy or Germany for the same period.

Exchange rate per US$1, 2011

| Cambodia | Riel | 4,005.000 |
|---|---|---|
| China | Yuan | 6.506 |
| Hong Kong | HK Dollar | 7.774 |
| Indonesia | Rupia | 8,545.000 |
| Japan | Yen | 81.919 |
| Malaysia | Ringgit | 3.031 |
| Philippines | Peso | 43.160 |
| Singapore | Singapore Dollar | 1.293 |
| South Korea | Won | 1,086.150 |
| Taiwan | Taiwan Dollar | 28.830 |
| Thailand | Baht | 30.279 |
| Vietnam | Dong | 20,690.000 |

*Source: XE-Universal Currency Converter*

The group of emerging countries in Asia shows yearly GDP per capita that are clearly less than USD 10,000 except the 2012 estimate for Malaysia (USD 9200). This list of emerging countries includes The People's Republic of China, Thailand, the Philippines, Indonesia, as well as Vietnam, Laos, and Cambodia. In these markets the GDP per capita for year 2012 ranges between USD 2,000–3,000 (Philippines, Indonesia, with Vietnam rapidly catching up) and USD 5,000–6,000 (China, Thailand). Laos and Cambodia are still very poor (USD 1,000).

The interviews we have conducted in Asia essentially reflect these income levels but it is fair to say that since we mostly interview people who shop at modern stores, our data involve the upper and middle classes, not the poor households and doesn't represent the average income groups of the countries. We generally measure family incomes so if in a country both husband and wife are working we count their combined income. If, as in Korea and Japan, the female is usually a housewife, the husband's salary is the only income that supports the household. In these two countries the average household income is generally equivalent to the husband's salary, which is around USD 4,000 (Korea) to 5,000 per month (Japan) or a little more. The households we interviewed in Hong

Kong, Singapore and Taipei (Taiwan) earn around USD 3,000 per month while the average salaries amount to USD 1,500 to 2000 (two wage earners most of the time plus some side business activities). For Taiwanese residents who live outside Taipei in the south of Taiwan, the incomes are about 15 percent less.

Average Household Income and Salary in US$, 2011

|  | Household Income | Salary | Legal Minimum Salary |
|---|---|---|---|
| Cambodia | 1,289 | 612 | 267 |
| China | 5,907 | 3,781 | 2,041 |
| Hong Kong | 27,014 | 18,529 | 5,526 |
| Indonesia | N/A | 4,619 | 1,437 |
| Japan | 61,814 | 52,491 | 15,692 |
| Malaysia | 14,651 | 4,132 | 2,772 |
| Philippines | 4,773 | 2,572 | 1,126 |
| Singapore | 69,877 | 15.498 | No law |
| South Korea | 43,703 | 41,652 | 7,871 |
| Taiwan | 37,259 | 18,189 | 7,193 |
| Thailand | 8,284 | 3,171 | 1,271 |
| Vietnam | 1,125 | 661 | 313 |

Source: Local National Statistics, National Wages and Productivities Commission

In developing countries, household monthly incomes are significantly lower. They can approach USD 1,000 in the main cities of China as well as in Bangkok, Thailand but can be 40 percent or 50 percent less in rural areas. In a city like Jakarta, Indonesia, monthly household income can be USD 800 and again around 40 percent less in other places of Indonesia, whereas in main cities of Laos and Cambodia the average household income would reach a few hundred dollars per month at best.

Families who shop at hypermarkets, supermarkets, or department stores in Asia dedicate a different proportion of their household income to food, garments, leisure, home interior, and other product categories. Broadly speaking, the customers in richer Asian countries (Japan, Korea, Hong Kong, Taiwan, Singapore) will spend about 20 percent of their income for food and a relatively low percentage on clothing and furnishing (less than 5 percent each) but higher expenditures for housing (20 percent), health (10-15 percent), leisure and cultural activities (10-15 percent). In the less-developed economies (Indonesia, Thailand, Philippines, China, Vietnam for instance) the ratios will be different with a higher proportion of income dedicated to food (approximately 30-35 percent), clothing (5-10 percent depending on the region and climate) and relatively less on housing (15 percent) or medical needs (less than 5 percent).

## Living arrangements

The typical family background is also quite simple to describe. In Japan and Korea, virtually all people feel they belong to the middle classes. Households in Japan or Korea are typically nuclear families, husband and wife with one or two children (more often two children in Korea and less so in Japan), and living in apartments. In these two countries, usually only one person has a paid occupation, and two-thirds of the time the housewife is the only person in charge of shopping for daily necessities. The children will live with their parents until their late twenties, early thirties, sometimes even if they have a job.

In Chinese markets (Hong Kong and Singapore but also Mainland China and Taiwan) housing is different. In the past, families used to live in houses but now more and more live in apartments, up to 80 percent in most cities of Mainland China. These apartments are mostly low rise and unsophisticated but about half of the Chinese shoppers we have interviewed own their apartment. The rest are tenants or live in company housing, sometimes owned by semi-public companies. The free housing sponsored by the state has almost disappeared. As for Hong Kong, more than 97 percent of the population resides in apartments.

In the same way as for Japan and Korea, the children in Chinese families will often live a long time in their parents' homes. This generates a large market since, when they have a job and pay virtually no rent, these young adults benefit from a high disposable income. A main difference however, between the Chinese territories and Japan or Korea is the role of women. A wife in Japan and Korea is a housewife but Chinese women work, even when married, in private or public companies, self-employment or public service. The main reason for this is necessity. In Chinese countries, women may not have career ambitions, but they need to work because households cannot survive well with one salary alone.

Southeast Asian countries are quite comparable to the Chinese example. In the past, families were extended and it was not uncommon to see three or sometimes four generations living under the same roof. A married couple would live in a house together with their children but also with the parents of the husband. In many cases the house itself would belong to the husbands' parents and this older generation would be taken care of by son and daughter-in-law, until their passing. Today however, families are more nuclear in Southeast Asia as in the rest of the world.

## Physical conditions in a market

Other than demographics, the natural and economic backgrounds have a direct impact on consumption and shopping. Climate and weather constitute a good example of this. In tropical countries you can live all year long with light clothes while in areas where winters are cold, such as parts of China, Japan and Korea, you will have to buy a certain amount of textiles in order to keep warm. In Beijing you will need woolen sweaters, warm boots, and coats; in Singapore, you won't.

When you build a home in a country that is prone to earthquakes, in Japan, Taiwan, and some zones of China for example, parts of the construction costs have to do with seismic standards. What is done to reinforce the structure of the building involves an extra cost; it is part of the budget. This demand exists by necessity, and has nothing to do with whether people are rich, old, or live in small families. If you go to shopping malls in Taiwan, chances are that you will see tents, gas stoves, flashlights, and lots of other outdoor gear in stores. This suggests outdoor activities and trekking, yet camping is not a dominant hobby in that country. Part of this particular demand comes from people who worry about seismic activity. They fear they may become homeless if there is an earthquake one day, and want to be ready with some kind of shelter.

Nature will impact shopping behavior and expenditures, so will macro-economic conditions stemming from local authorities or the local economy. There can be a government decision to reduce or increase a tax to encourage people to shop in certain ways. If a government in Asia wants to protect the small family-run stores, there may be rules against opening large hypermarkets in certain parts of cities. Conversely, where a government allows "big box" supercenters to open in the cities, you will find lots of hypermarkets downtown. Whichever way, there will be a huge impact on the shopping behaviors in the parts of towns concerned.

Local authorities may also decide that the residential zones in the center of big cities like in Shanghai are becoming too crowded and that residents of some districts have to relocate to the suburbs. This in turn, will involve the construction of new housing complex in the satellite towns. Since more and more families will relocate there, it will generate new demand for various electric appliances, furniture, and home improvements in general. From a macro-economic standpoint, the shopping needs in the suburb are modified. Instead of sleepy towns, the satellite cities become bustling areas where people will now buy refrigerators, television sets, sofas and tables, paint, and wallpaper much more than average. If you are a chain store of the relevant product category, it makes sense to consider opening retail outlets in these areas, whatever the demographic data.

Physical conditions at the macroeconomic level can also be produced by constraints other than decisions by the authorities, such as the cost structure on a market segment. If we keep the example of home improvement above we can point out two significant differences between Asia and the West.

When you buy a new apartment in many Asian countries, you only acquire what is called an "empty shell." While the apartment has plumbing and electricity, you still have to install flooring, bathroom and kitchen fixtures, appliances, and wall tiles, in addition to paint and furniture, so you purchase separately more elements than you would in the West. It's a difference of market structure. The second difference occurs when you want to renovate your home. In the West, decorating or renovating has become a hobby and many middle-class people love do-it-yourself (DIY). In the Far East, this is not so. People invoke cultural reasons to explain this and suggest that Asians aren't comfortable painting walls or assembling pieces of furniture, therefore the DIY market is not significant. In fact, many Asian males, not unlike Western males in the field of DIY, like to have an electric drill and a toolbox. The difference lies mostly in the macroeconomic conditions in the markets: the cost structure of goods and services. Since in Western countries it is expensive to ask a professional to install hardwood flooring for your living room or to come and decorate your windows with new curtains, people in Europe or the U.S. will often buy the materials and do the home improvement they have in mind for themselves.

In most countries in the Far East on the other hand, using the service of a local designer or a contractor is relatively inexpensive. Asian customers will therefore ask a professional to visit their home, discuss the renovation project and offer a quotation. More often than not, when they buy materials, end customers actually visit the retailers together with their designer or contractor; the latter pays the retailer for the items bought since the quotation includes the materials. Asian customers suppose that the contractor has a commission from the retailer (in a market like Hong Kong it's typically 10 percent or a little less); but since the customers see the price paid in the store is the same as the marked price and not more, they don't mind.

In part, the DIY market is pre-determined by the cost benefit consideration: it feels quite inexpensive to use the service of a professional for home improvement in Asia. For this reason (and not because Asians are uncomfortable using a hammer or a screwdriver) the demand in the Far East is more Buy It Yourself than Do It Yourself. The challenge for modern trade retailers then, is to adjust the product assortment: if less people do actual DIY, the stores may need to offer fewer tools but more decoration styles, organize fewer DIY clinics and "how to" sessions, but display more end results and showrooms that inspire shoppers. They also need to adjust the service offer, and to compete with local contractors by providing total solutions, including their own designers and their own decoration centers.

The market situation, due in this case to the cost structure of services, generates a physical condition that will have an impact on what happens at retail. In a market like China, when customers buy homes, they will judge most home improvement chains not simply on the product range or prices but on service, such as the quality of the installation or renovation work offered by the chain.

There are many other physical conditions that determine shopping. It can be as simple as the general economic growth. If people feel the country is doing well, they will gladly shop more. As a contractor puts it, "If the real estate business is good, most customers would renovate their entire house, if not, they'll just want to do other small jobs." Even the local stock market has an effect: when it's up, people in Asia will sell shares and make money, which at least in part, they will use for shopping. The housing structure is also a macroeconomic determinant. In a market where 98 percent of the families live in apartments, for example, the demand for gardening has to be minimal.

## Local culture

We've seen that demographics and physical conditions may differ from country to country in Asia. In many respects those factors that pre-determine shopping behaviors can be measured and quantified quite realistically. Through surveys, we can evaluate the age and income groups of shoppers; we can know if a city is being transformed and how many households are planned to relocate from downtown to specific areas in the suburbs for instance. And since natural conditions are long-term factors, we can realistically evaluate them too. The markets are different but we can still take into account the demographics, the regulations and the economy, as well as climate.

The other element that will influence consumption and shopping is culture, such as the general habits in a country or in a family, the social beliefs, the ways people communicate, and so forth. In this respect, we can make the case that in the Far East, countries are somewhat similar, and that culturally they have lots of similarities when it comes to shopping behavior.

Religion could be considered as a major cultural trait, but it is not really one. First, there is no strong monotheist religion in Asia, apart from Muslims who are a minority in most countries (more on this in the further chapters). Second, even if Asians are Taoist, Buddhists, or Shinto, or believe in multiple gods, those religions and beliefs do not really conflict with each other as far as shopping is concerned. While we'll talk about Asian Muslim shoppers later in this book, let's just say for now that essentially, Asian Muslims tend to spend a little less than other people in a same country.

Another point about Asian culture relates to superstitions. People have beliefs about what is a good omen or not, and will consult fortune tellers, books about astrology, or go to temples and shrines to ask for various blessings. This happens in all Asian countries and is much more important than just flipping through the horoscope pages in the morning paper in the West. Even highly educated Asians tend to remain superstitious for life, but here too, the impact on shopping behaviors is not very important.

In fact, there is one basic philosophy in Asian culture, which does have an effect on how shoppers and store employees behave. It applies to Japan and Korea, in Southeast Asia, in Hong Kong, Taiwan and China, and can be summarized by the word *Confucianism*. This book is not about Confucius but it's probably a good thing to dedicate a few lines about the ethics that he developed (Confucius, *The Analects*). First, Confucianism is not a religion; it is about social behavior. It also doesn't have much to do with beliefs like ancestor-worship, cults, or with superstitions. Confucius,who was Chinese, lived 2,500 years ago and propagated a philosophy that over the centuries spread all over Asia. It is by no means a "Chinese only" ethic. To make it simple, we can say there are three moral principles in Asia that reflect Confucianism:

**Work hard** from a young age (starting with school) up to adult life.

**Respect authority,** i.e., your father, your teacher, your boss, but also by extension, your customer.

**Maintain harmony,** avoid situations that are embarrassing for others and for yourself (don't make people lose face, for instance).

This heritage belongs to all Asian countries. Koreans—even when they are Christians, Japanese—even if they are Shinto, Malaysians—even Muslim Malays, and Thai or Vietnamese Buddhists will behave in society with these principles in mind, although it is not necessarily called Confucianism. We will see in the coming pages that these values have an effect on shopping and are actually common to all the markets in the Far East.

Let's summarize the three factors that impact shopping behavior—demographics, physical conditions, and culture—with a simple example: buying food, such as beef or chicken. Based on the demographics (income, number of children at home), a mother can decide to buy some beef because it is at the right price for the family budget and is nutritious. If she is a Chinese Malaysian however, she may buy chicken if she believes that beef should not be eaten; conversely, an Asian housewife in another country may think that eating chicken causes arthritis, so based on her cultural beliefs she may or may not purchase it. Moreover, if there is an alert on bird flu or mad cow disease, which in this case involves the macroeconomic environment, the mother will not buy poultry or beef when she does her grocery shopping.

# 2

# Seeing Is Believing

IN ORDER to explain what we mean by the notion of "seeing is believing" in Asia, it may be worthwhile to start with a small anecdote.

The scene takes place in Macao, Lisboa Hotel, at one of the numerous tables where casino players flock and hope to beat the odds and if possible to become rich overnight. The room is vast. In the distance you can see some of the slot machines where various types of people are playing. And there are also lots of people just looking on.

In the middle of the vast room are several tables where 6 to 10 players are seated or standing, some dressed in tuxedos, and some are less formal. At one of these tables is a young-looking Englishman, maybe 35 years old. His name is Andrew. He has been playing roulette for some time and, judging from the chips he has in front of him, he is here to bet large sums of money. For quite some time now, he has been winning.

Little by little, the other players and a few Macao people who came here to look around, notice this English player. People start to flock behind Andrew from other parts of the room and some from the slot machine area. Standing behind, they watch him play. The Macao and other Asian onlookers stare intensely; their eyes glance at the beads, the chips, then they look at Andrew and wait for the result. He wins again.

Some Chinese start to play the same colors as Andrew at this table, while others try the exact same numbers. And those numbers win again. Nobody shouts however. There is no burst of joy; no particular reaction can be noticed. It seems like every onlooker is captivated and focused.

There is now a significant crowd around this table, mostly composed of Macao players and other Asians. This continues for a while and, at some point, Andrew decides to stop; he has been lucky tonight so far and perhaps does not want to take too much risk. Some of the Chinese players, who played the same odds as Andrew, and won, are slightly disappointed. However, none of them tries to "touch" Andrew as if he were a miracle man or to ask him for his secrets. They don't believe that touching someone who wins at the roulette will make them winners, too. What they believe is that if he is winning with these numbers and colors, then it is worth doing exactly the same thing. Now, one of the Chinese players, dressed not particularly well, approaches Andrew and gives him a banknote.

A tip! A way to say, "Thank you for making me win." By politeness, Andrew accepts it; he certainly doesn't need a tip but sees no reason to offend the Asian player and thanks him with a smile before leaving.

This is a true story. Andrew is a real person, a friend of ours. What happened here is an example of Asian beliefs, and it illustrates a few points about behavior in the Far East as compared with Westerners. In the West, a player's attitude in a casino would often relate to statistics, even if he is not fully conscious of it. For instance, a European or a North American would stick to the same numbers or the same slot machine and would believe that if he or she plays long enough on this particular machine or set of numbers, there will finally come a time when probabilities will be on his side and he will win the jackpot. The feeling then, is that statistically it makes sense to play the same way for a long time, but he would not necessarily want to just play the same bets as someone who is *currently* winning.

In the Far East the reaction, quite superstitious in a way, is more direct and more visual. If Asians actually see that someone in front of them is winning right now, by acting in a specific way, they will want to do the same thing, right now, as well. This process is present in all Asian countries, at varying degrees but does not depend much upon education or level of income. This example is about something that is *visible*. You *see* in front of you the casino player winning, and then it becomes a solid truth that whatever he does is the right thing to do.

## The importance of observation

There is something else with the casino anecdote. Some people feel they won thanks to Andrew and want to thank him, in a quite spontaneous way, since no one took time to think whether "doing the same as Andrew" is a good idea or not. People just did it, and then thanked him briskly.

This notion of acting quickly and decisively is a point that is not well understood about the Far East. In the West, people tend to think that Asians are patient and philosophical. This is not entirely true. There is a Chinese saying, which we think is enlightening: "If you plant a stick in the ground, you have to see its shadow right away."

It denotes the sense of observation, you have to *see* the shadow, it is visible, it is beyond uncertainty, but also implies a certain level of impatience. You must see the shadow immediately. Whatever the action, the result has to be quick. This notion of urgency is representative of many customers in the region.

An Asian female buying a skin-softening cream might be convinced if she tries a sample and quickly feels the softening effect on her skin. If she is told it is a treatment that requires a few weeks, she may be much less inclined to buy it because the effect would not be perceptible quickly. She would need time to judge the result, to feel and to see it.

In a restaurant in Asia, be it upscale or a small family-run eatery, waiters make a point of regularly looking at tables and guests to observe whether the customers have finished a plate and if they judge this is the case, promptly remove the dish. Many Westerners have been surprised, if not frustrated at times during a meal in restaurants in Asia, when a waiter suddenly comes to take your plate, and bring new clean ones, although the customers barely finished enjoying the dish. This is not because waiters have been trained to remove plates and speed up the meal. It is not because they want diners to leave the table as soon as possible so other clients could occupy the table. The point is not rotation or profitability. It is simply that for an Asian waiter, the leftovers should not appear on a table; it is not tidy. The waiter sees when a plate is almost finished, and judges that the right thing to do is to quickly replace it with a new one. He sees and takes a quick action.

An Asian retailer also lives and loves this notion of urgency. Whenever an Asian traditional vendor sells something to a client, he is experiencing this quick result, in the form of money and of profit margin. It is the same with international chains or any modern trade. For example, whenever an Asian supermarket retailer changes some facings or sets up a gondola end, to showcase a product, he or she will check out the sales at the end of the same day. Many professional retailers in Asia tell me that one of their joys at work is to see right away the results of whatever actions they implement.

## Observation and perception

In Asia, everybody looks at everybody. This is done in a soft way and does not involve any verbal remarks. People will look at each other when they meet for the first time and gauge what is their respective age, or which ethnic background they are, or estimate whether they are city dwellers or live in the countryside.

Observation plays a role in shopping situations too. At retail, we encounter comments such as this example.

" . . . that day I was just wearing sandals, the store staff saw me
(not wearing leather shoes) and did not show me respect."

(Thai female, 31 years old, department store, Bangkok)

The issue here is that the shopper belongs to mid-upper class and as a reasonably well-to-do person in an up-market department store, she feels she lost face, not because she did something wrong but because she was perceived as rather poor by a sales girl who judged her in the blink of an eye.

Here is a second example:

*"I don't want to buy underwear [in this store] because this department is too close to the check-out counters, I'd feel embarrassed."*

(Japanese female shopper, 34 years old, hypermarket, Osaka)

This Japanese lady feels uneasy not because she requires a fitting room or because she hesitates on the quality of the products; she would gladly buy some of the items. But she feels a kind of bashfulness if she buys panties while being scrutinized by dozens of pairs of eyes. All those shoppers queuing at the checkout counters a few meters away have nothing else to do than look around at what is happening in the store. Observation is important in Asia; so is the way you are perceived.

*". . . I wanted to ask a [staff-member] where the battery department is but I didn't, they looked so busy."*

(Chinese male shopper, 43 years old, category killer)

This Chinese client is looking for technical goods and could ask store employees for help but what he sees is that the employees are all engaged in logistics works, removing cartons on the floor, or filling shelves. Based on what he can discern, they seem to have little time available and his emotional response is that he should not disrupt their work.

In Korea too, all the visible elements have an emotional importance although it may be considered superfluous. Shopping at a hypermarket in Seoul is a more upscale experience than in most cities in the West. From the moment you enter the parking facility you will see employees greeting the visitors and guiding the cars, almost like valet parking. The visit remains upscale once in store, with the bright lights, perfect cleanliness, and an array of tasting opportunities to keep the shoppers interested, pampered, and motivated. At the non-food sections, the product displays provide more of a department store feel, than what a hypermarket normally does. The experience remains upscale in terms of service too, since the Korean customers can find resting areas with bench, chairs, and water fountains, as well as child-care zones with playgrounds for kids, so housewives can do their shopping conveniently.

All this could seem unnecessary in the case of a hypermarket, because to get into a car park you don't need staff members waving at you and you can do your shopping even if there is no bench, free samples, or water fountain. The point is customers feel that, with the bench and the playground, the store has sacrificed part of the sales area in order to improve the comfort of shoppers, and by giving away free samples and paying for parking valets, the store does a lot to accommodate the customers.

The shoppers see for themselves tangible proof that the retailer values them. They don't necessarily perceive that, with the resting area, they actually stay longer in store and tend to increase the amount of purchase per shopping visit. Or that if you see lots of food samples to taste, chances are you will appreciate some and then purchase a few of those. The shoppers mostly feel they are taken care of and are grateful.

## A few keys to better understand Asian shoppers

In the same way that the casino players echoed what Andrew was doing, in daily life people in Asia will also tend to do the same as others.

At any street in Shanghai, even if there is a red light for pedestrians, you will see that if one person undertakes to cross the street, several others will walk along and do the same.

In virtually all Asian cities, if you stroll in some back streets, you will discover numerous small family-run stores selling food, stationery, and clothes. Some of those family businesses are providing services, such as restaurants, laundry, and hair styling. Someone who recently moved into the neighborhood and needs a haircut will notice two barber shops next to each other, one being very busy and the other having almost no customers.

Why is it so? Is one hair stylist more successful because she is nicer than the other, works harder, or is more fashionable? Actually both appear nice and hard working. In each case the stylists don't chat very much with the customers and the haircuts are very standard, their style is "no frills." Is one outlet larger and more spacious? No, both operate in 50 or 60 square meters. Perhaps it is because one is cheaper than the other. No, they offer the same price range. We could imagine lots of different reasons, maybe superstition, if the location of one outlet is a bad omen; or maybe one barbershop has a better heating system or provides better air conditioning.

More than the technical reason why one shop is more successful than the other, the point is this: Asians do not talk much to each other spontaneously about recommendations, nor ask comments regarding stores and services. So if an Asian person comes to live in this particular neighborhood, he or she will make an educated guess based on what can be seen, not by asking others.

In Asia you are more likely to become a customer at the successful hair stylist (even if it means you have to wait for your turn whenever you go there) than at the other one, simply because everybody else goes there. The same is true for a large store. If two hypermarkets or department stores operate next to one another, a potential customer will look at which outlet has more customers and will go and shop there. The rationale is that, if so many people shop at that store, they must have a good reason.

## It's Confucianism again

We pointed out that observation and a kind of behavioral mimicry play a role in daily life as well as the need for acting quickly without being assertive. There is a common denominator to all this—Confucianism as we briefly stated in the introduction.

Confucius was trying to elevate the moral standards of the leaders of his time. He was not very successful at being an advisor to the prince but over the centuries, the values he taught percolated among the general population in China and then in the rest of the continent. We mentioned three core values: work hard, respect authority, and preserve harmony.

One probably doesn't need to emphasize the view that Asians are hard workers so we won't elaborate on this, except for two remarks. Far East people are not robots; an Asian worker will appreciate a rest; an Asian child will want to have fun outdoors with friends or play video games at home, like any other kid, but work comes first and children are taught that homework comes first.

The second remark is that hard work does not necessarily mean high productivity and does not mean intense labor. It simply means that Asians will work long hours because the number of hours of labor is quantifiable. A student will write a long essay for instance, because the number of pages can be calculated (whereas the intensity of the long hours writing the essay or the quality of the work are not easy to measure).

The Asian respect for authority is also quite well known. This precept starts at childhood. Asian children learn to show respect to the parents and to elders. It continues at school, respect for the teacher, and at the office, respect toward the boss. Unless the authority holder is extremely unfair and ferocious, typical Asians will comply. The concept of harmony is also interesting; it has to be visible. Unlike Westerners who may have a clash, say what they have to say, and then move on, Asians will avoid confrontation because it disrupts harmony. In Asia, whatever a person may think, he or she will act in a sociable way, in order to be in harmony with the rest of the society.

Does Confucianism provide a key to understanding the shoppers and their behavior? Let's quickly review some of our previous examples. The Chinese male shopper looking for batteries will not interrupt the employees in order to have some information about batteries, because what he sees is that the store staff are very busy. Seeing is believing: they are working hard.

The lady with sandals has another problem. As a rich customer she is supposed to convey authority but she doesn't look so rich today. In the eye of the sales girl, this customer is not so much an authority because she wears sandals. You need to look like the authority.

The new resident in the neighborhood will opt for the successful beauty salon or the crowded department store not as a copycat, but because it reflects the harmony of that time and place as she sees it.

You might consider that the few pedestrians in Shanghai, crossing the road when they shouldn't, are not respecting authority and are not in harmony. In fact the authority has to be visible. If there is no policeman or no traffic agent in the vicinity, there is no authority that you can see, so no authority to obey. "The sky is high, the Emperor is far," says a well-known Chinese proverb. How about harmony though? Harmony also has to be visible and has a social validation. During the time when these few pedestrians cross the street, they are together. During these few seconds, they create their own social harmony. Within their own little bubble, they are in harmony.

Confucianism illustrates a set of simple values that are shared by Asians from Korea and Japan, to China and all the way south to Indonesia irrespective of the religious beliefs. In terms of shopping, what we observe is that a shopper's judgment is based on direct sight. Customers' perceptions don't come so much from hearsay (because Asian people will not comment spontaneously to each other about products and stores), nor from store staff advice (because one cannot be sure about the reliability). Thus, Asian shoppers rely on what they can see for themselves. One could say they are first-degree. They see that a store is crowded; therefore it must be a good store. They see the employees are busy; therefore one should not interrupt them. However, saying Asian customers are first-degree is not enough. What they need to see also has to be measurable in some way. Qualitative criteria or moral values (a store offering a line of fair-trade products or pledging to limit the use of plastic bags, for instance) are not sufficient to motivate an Asian customer. The shoppers need to quantify the benefits.

## Seeing—something measurable

We emphasize the notion that in Asia, what counts is what you see. Busy people have to look busy. Managers have to look authoritative. Within a group of Asian people the group has to look harmonious. What you see has to be clear, obvious, and ideally it has to be measurable and quantifiable.

For example, in China, a supermarket offers a promotion on eggs for a limited period of time. Immediately a few shoppers will notice it and queue for this special offer. Others will then see the queue and will wait in line as well. In no time a snowball effect takes place and there are long queues of shoppers of all ages waiting in line to buy a few eggs. You see, and you act quickly, especially since others do, too. The point here is that the notion of seeing and deciding promptly is something measurable. You judge and decide in a few seconds.

An Asian mother has to buy a notebook or a workbook for her child for school. Given the choice of two notebooks, she will probably select the larger because bigger is better. This is measurable. When she was at school herself, she had the feeling that it was better to write a great many pages; it looked positive because it represented hard work. If this mother has a job, she may well work long hours at the office, because the number of hours is visible and measurable and it is judged positively. The intensity or the efficiency of the long hours will be secondary. What counts is the volume that people can see—the number of seconds to make a decision, the number of pages, the number of hours at the office, and the size of a crowd at the hair stylist. Things that are quantifiable will matter.

When an Asian mother cooks a meal for the family (we refer to home cooking, not to a microwave dish nor instant noodles), she will observe her family: Do they eat with pleasure; do they eat quickly, or slowly; do they eat everything and finish their plates. She will not expect someone to say this is delicious, but she will rely on observation. If family members or guests ask for more, this is quantifiable.

Hualien, Taiwan, is the "city of marble," where 8 to 10 million tons

are quarried every year. If you enter one of the dozens of stores selling coasters, letter openers, and other marble objects and if you ask for
advice, local retailers will recommend green marble. Vendors could give
you various reasons. They could say that green is the color of jade and
it provides a feeling of wealth. They could allege that green color brings
good luck, or estimate that the green hue and various shades of veins are
more beautiful than other colors. In fact, the retailers' explanation will
stem from a simple, and measurable, reason: solidity. They will explain
that white, red, or brownish marble is softer, while green marble is harder
and more resistant. It doesn't really matter if this is true or not. What
matters is that vendors relate to the most quantifiable criterion they can
find. You can measure more easily the solidity of a mineral than you can
measure it's beauty or it's ability to bring luck.

We did an interesting survey some time ago about wine differentiation,
with Asian respondents who are not familiar with wine and spirits. We
probed attitudes toward three bottles of red wine, identical in every aspect
but one. All three bottles had the same shape and capacity and were made
of the same glass; the liquid had the same red hue; the labels had the same
design and the same color codes; the price points were identical; and the
three bottles were presented at eye level in the same manner in random
order. The only difference was the grape variety. We had one cabernet
sauvignon, one gamay, and one merlot. The Asian subjects knew nothing
about wine and nothing about the various types of grapes used. Some had
heard the word *chateau*. That was the extent of their knowledge. The test
did not involve smelling the wines or tasting, and the conditions were that
the subjects could not ask a store staff member for advice.

Therefore, when asked to select a bottle, the respondents could only
differentiate among the *words* merlot or cabernet sauvignon or gamay.
If you think the preferred bottle was the cabernet sauvignon, you are
right. More than 45 percent preferred it, nearly as much as the others
combined. Gamay ranked second with 31 percent of the votes and merlot was last, at 23 percent. One or two points are interesting here. First,
gamay is rarely on the market in Asia. Respondents said they liked the

name "gamay" because it was easy to read and to remember (it was the same for the minority who liked merlot). Second, one may think that cabernet sauvignon is preferred simply because of exposure. After all, even though they are not wine experts, the interviewees probably saw bottles of cabernet sauvignon at supermarkets and perhaps they remembered it unconsciously. But if this was the case, the same would be true for merlot, as it is also very well represented in stores, at least at supermarkets. Besides, a six-letter word like merlot will benefit from larger typeface on a label and will be more visible and memorable than a 17-letter word. So exposure is not the answer. However, the main point is still related to the number of letters: cabernet sauvignon is preferred by nearly half of the respondents *because* of its long name. The long name "looks delicious;" the long name "sounds like it's a good grape." This is because respondents are focused on quantity. If the name contains more letters, the wine probably contains more fragrance, more components, more taste. This is first-degree thinking; the bigger the better. Since cabernet sauvignon actually consists of two words, it's like thinking that a wine with a double name will have twice the flavor. If you think in terms of quality you would probably dispute this and say that the taste, flavors, mellowness, and so forth will depend on the specifics of each grape variety, but the thinking here is not about quality; it's about quantity.

## Believing, being tricked, or missing a chance

Customers are sometimes victims of the "seeing is believing" notion. At a traditional market, be it in China, Malaysia, the Philippines, or elsewhere in the Far East, there will be vegetable merchants trying to deceive their customers about the net weight of the produce. If you buy 1 kilo of Chinese cabbage at the market, the scale shows it does weigh 1 kilo. As a customer, you can see it and it also feels heavy. The Asian customer will be satisfied that she is getting value for money. However, this kilogram mark is often due, in part, to water that was sprayed or sprinkled on the vegetable. Of course, it is done in order to make the produce look nice and fresh but also to increase the net weight.

In Japan, supermarkets and general merchandise stores may offer a specific food item like tempura to be displayed after 11 a.m. At 10:50 a.m. housewives will expect to see the store sign stating a specific message such as "tempura will start in 10 minutes." Indeed, tempura displays will appear on time and the Japanese shopper will feel reassured that since it is timely, it is probably fresh. She will not wonder too much whether the shrimp used are a day old because seeing is believing. It is visibly on the shelf just in time.

Asians can be deceived in a shopping situation if they rely on seeing-is-believing, but they can also miss opportunities because this notion doesn't encourage boldness and doesn't encourage a leap of faith. Think about warehouse clubs. Member club retailers like Costco, Sam's Club, or Makro are established in many Asian countries. The concept is simple: you buy a yearly membership and as a member, you can benefit from good products at cheap prices. In some cases those chains aim for small businesses, restaurant owners, and small retailers who buy in bulk (often called HORECA, hotel, restaurant, caterers), but in fact almost any Asian household can buy from member clubs in Asia.

The challenge for these chains is the initial stage. The retailer has to convince Asian shoppers that they should pay in order to *become* a member. The issue is not only to offer very attractive prices, to provide a differentiated assortment, or a great shopping experience. It is actually more basic and more first degree. Asian customers feel that, as clients, they are supporting a store when they shop there, so their thinking is, "Why should I pay you for doing you a favor?"

The potential shopper has not seen nor experienced Sam's Club or the Costco warehouse store yet, and does not automatically realize that she should pay for a membership. The concept of participating by paying a fee on the overall expenses *first*, in exchange for cost benefits *later* does not match the seeing-is-believing attitude. You cannot quantify the benefit at the beginning stage because you cannot see the store yet. So in Asian countries, the warehouse chains have to adjust their membership fee system. Since customers want to be able to measure, the retail chains have to offer a low membership fee and to publicize that this fee can be refunded at any time, with no questions asked. Otherwise everybody loses.

Product return is also an issue that has to do with seeing-is-believing. After you have made a purchase, you may experience disappointment with some items you bought. In the case of food, it may have a very bad taste. If it is non-food, the product may be damaged or have some kind of malfunction and you want to return it. In the West it is not always simple to have the item replaced or to be reimbursed. "Your money back, no questions asked," is not always easy to achieve, and is complicated, but Western shoppers will try, on the grounds that they have the right to return a product.

In Asia, many customers will tend not to go to the exchange and refund desk in the first place, because this would be a visible expression of conflict. It's embarrassing and there is a risk that someone will lose face. And, if they do go to the product return desk, in many cases the store staff will try to avoid a return. By culture, some Asian employees will ask the shoppers if they could still accept the product, alleging that the malfunction is not that bad. Or they may say that the original pack is damaged so the product is not as good as new any more and cannot be returned. In the case of fresh food, (e.g., a pack of sausages) a customer might go to the exchange and refund desk and explain that she bought the product the day before without noticing that the "best before date" was expired, and she would like to return it. However, the staff will perhaps claim that the product was bought, not yesterday but a week ago, at a time when the expiry date was not reached. If the customer shows the receipt of yesterday, the staff may very well think this is not the relevant receipt. In other words, nobody thinks the other is truthful and the product return can become unpleasant. If the issue is not serious, some Asian customers will decide not to insist because they don't want to be perceived as troublemakers.

Sometimes, shoppers do insist though. When we conduct satisfaction surveys in stores, some customers who have had a bad experience with exchange and refund, will even ask our surveyors to go with them to the product return desk so as to express their complaints. Our interviewers don't take sides of course, but the real issue is that store employees sometimes will make a point of saving a few dollars, and end up making the customers upset. For some employees, saving two dollars on behalf of the store is a measurable achievement, but losing a customer is not tangible so it feels less important. This is not good business. Many satisfied customer households in Asia will spend the equivalent of $750 each year at their food store. The staff in charge of product return may feel proud for not reimbursing, but the store is better off giving a customer the benefit of the doubt instead of saving the price of a sausage.

## The principle of charity

There is another element about customer attitude, which is not specific to Asians but is worth mentioning here since this book compares satisfaction and dissatisfaction. From time to time we will see that for example, 55 or 60 percent of the customers are satisfied with a certain aspect of their shopping experience, in which case we may feel this is quite good or at least, not too bad.

However, when customers shop a particular store, they believe that they have a good reason to do so. If you ask them if they feel the store offers good prices or a good ambiance, or anything else, many will tend to answer it is satisfactory because saying the opposite would seem somewhat illogical ("If I don't like this store, why is it that I shop here in the first place?"). Of course shoppers can express discontent but they also feel a need to answer in a way that sounds rational.

There is a concept, called the principle of charity that, in a nutshell, says the human brain looks for rationality. It is easy to illustrate this in markets where advertisements are regulated for some product categories, such as for example, a country where ads for confections require some kind of statement about health or obesity. For instance, TV commercials would thus showcase some snacks or candies and at the end of the ad, a tagline would say you should be careful about calories. The audience would see:

1. A message that says "eat this chocolate bar."
2. A tagline that says "don't eat too many calories."

With the principle of charity, the customer would unconsciously try to make sense of these conflicting messages and reach the logical conclusion that "it's OK to eat this chocolate bar *because* it doesn't contain too many calories;" otherwise, the ad would not tell me to eat it while paying attention to calories. This is counter-productive for the regulators, because in a way it encourages people to eat these confections and thus to somewhat damage their health. But it is the way for a customer to find rationality.

The same applies in a judgment about a shopping experience. I am rational. If I shop this store it's because I appreciate it. Therefore I tend to answer that I'm satisfied. So if a store survey shows that 55–60 percent of the customers are satisfied about something, you cannot automatically conclude this is good news. Additional input will be needed.

What we learned about Asian shoppers and their ways of thinking: customers and retailers in the Far East react in particular to what they see, and what they see has to be quantifiable quickly.

Let's now have a look at a hypermarket and visit it together with a local family.

# 3

# A Visit to a Store

BIG STORES and malls in Asia with hypermarkets and category killers can open in downtown or basically any part of a city. However, regulations in many Asian countries have been evolving. In order to protect small family-run stores, the zoning laws tend to hamper the opening of large outlets inside urban areas, especially in the case of food retail.

The main difference between shopping centers in Asia and Western countries is space allocation. Being located in town, Asian malls are not as huge as the ones at the outskirts of cities in the U.S. or Europe. In Asia, a four-floor downtown shopping center does not necessarily have hundreds of stores, but just two dozen small shops with a main anchor, a hypermarket, and perhaps just one category killer (furniture, electronics, toys, etc.) as co-anchor.

Space within the building is also allocated differently from the West. In Asia the hypermarket is likely to occupy levels two and three, and shoppers go up or down to buy all the things they want. In Western countries, the concept is to operate on just one level.

Space allocation for the parking lot is different too, depending on what type of vehicle customers use. In Korea, Thailand, or Japan, the shoppers most likely will come by car but if you are in Taiwan or Vietnam, customers may come to the shopping center by motorcycle, and in Mainland China, most will go by public bus. Only a few shoppers will use bicycles. Despite the cliché, the Chinese do not use bicycles all the time. In Singapore, Malaysia or Indonesia, the means or transportation are variable, cars, subways, pickup taxis or minivans (Indonesia) are possible as well as walking, because some shoppers prefer to go on foot when reasonably possible.

## A typical shopping trip

A visit to a shopping destination, as commonly experienced in Asia, could be described as follows. A typical customer would be a young lady in her early thirties, married with one child. Let's call her Suzy.

It's is early afternoon on a Sunday. Suzy is in the shopping center on the ground floor, with her five-year-old boy. The place is getting quite crowded and she is worried that her husband will have a difficult time finding her. Her husband is in the same building, but still in the parking facility. They came by car and the parking lot seemed full, but they did not go to another store and didn't just drive back home. Suzy and their son went to the store while her husband stayed in the car and circled around, until he found space to park the vehicle.

While circling, her husband thinks that even though they are in the habit of shopping at this hypermarket, there is another one not far from here and they probably should go there, instead of wasting time and gasoline trying to find a spot at the car park. He doesn't like the entrance of the parking lot anyway, because it's quite narrow and he's always worried that he might scratch the car when driving in.

Two floors up, Suzy is in the shopping gallery located at ground floor and walks along the various types of small stores, some fashion retailers selling affordable garments, sportswear, or mobile phones and consumer electronics, and a few small outlets offering accessories, watches, and decoration items.

## Shopping gallery and food court

The stores around Suzy are of all types, but mostly for non-food items. They have a small sales area, between 50–100 square meters, are clean, and there is lots of activity. If the visitors see animation and momentum they will be in the mood to visit and to buy. Like 75 percent of the shoppers, Suzy buys products from the non-food shops from time to time, but if she does, it is more likely to be before shopping at the hypermarket. There is also a food court, but it is somewhat different than the ones found in the U.S. or Europe. Generally speaking the ambiance in Asia for a food court is very casual except for money transactions: customers pay with coupons or with a prepaid card that they buy at the reception desk and not by cash or credit card.

For Suzy's son, the food court is always fun. He enjoys going to the counter to get a prepaid card and then choosing the dishes he likes and proudly paying with the card. He also enjoys going to the counter after the meal to reclaim the card value that was not spent. Once in a while, the family has lunch at the food court before going to shop at the hypermarket. Sometimes they go to the fast food restaurants that are at the ground floor as well. All are inexpensive and clean. Cleanliness is much better than at traditional markets, and the clean environment is actually a strength that customers like Suzy have in mind about food courts at shopping malls. Cleanliness is even a stronger factor than the taste or the value for money.

However, today the family is not having lunch here. Generally in Asia about two-thirds of the customers of a shopping center use the food court from time to time, but very few do so systematically. During weekdays, the food court customers are mostly white-collar employees who work in the vicinity, not just shoppers in the mall. On a typical Saturday or Sunday, only about 8 or 9 percent of customers who come for their grocery shopping will also have lunch or a snack at the food court, but that's enough for the food stalls to run profitably. The quick service or fast food restaurants, on the other hand are not always very profitable at shopping centers, but from a shopping mall point of view the food court (preferably with quick service restaurants) is considered as a must have.

When we interview Asians about their shopping intentions in the case of a *new* shopping mall that is going to open within the next 8 to 10 months, we want to know what kinds of outlets should be in the shopping center, other than the hypermarket or the department store that will be the main destination. About 70 percent of respondents say that they will be more likely to shop there if the shopping center has a food court. Asians like to eat or snack at various times of the day and if 8 to 10 percent of the 30,000 to 40,000 visitors who will shop there during the week use the food court, that is a fairly large number of users.

Other than the food court, the shopping gallery is also more than welcome by the shoppers, even when it consists only of a few dozen stores selling various specialties. Nearly 80 percent of the target customers will be more likely to come to shop at the hypermarket if there is a shopping gallery. Why not 100 percent? The remaining 20 percent consists of two groups. About 12 to 13 percent are just indifferent. They simply intend to do their grocery shopping and they don't care whether a shopping gallery will be there. A small fraction—6 to 8 percent—say they would be *less* likely to come to the shopping mall, if it offers a shopping gallery or a food court. These tend to be male. They belong to the same age groups as the other shoppers; they earn the same level of income, are married in the same proportion as the others, but their needs are generally more simple and direct. It is a matter of going to a store and buying the things they want. To some of these Asian males, the food court and the shopping gallery are perceived as places that will make the shopping destination too crowded, where they'll waste time, and they feel they'll be tempted to buy on impulse products or foods they don't really intend to buy.

Despite these few customers, the vast majority of shoppers, like Suzy, are in favor of food courts and shopping galleries in a shopping center. Today however, her objective is purely to go shopping at the hypermarket. Let's follow her and visit this hypermarket one floor up.

## The hypermarket

In order to reach the second floor, Suzy has to find the moving sidewalk also called autowalk or travelator. A lift or an escalator would not be very user-friendly because hypermarket shoppers use a trolley and a rolling walkway makes it easy to bring the shopping carts up or down a ramp safely. Some old-fashioned shopping centers in some Asian countries still have ramps made of concrete with no automatic travelators, but this is now quite rare.

Suzy has been here often, but it's always a challenge to find the travelator, which is at the end corner of the shopping gallery. Suzy thinks this is because the best areas are allocated to the tenants of the shopping gallery and the autowalk can be remote since shoppers will have to find it anyway. Like about 12 to 15 percent of shoppers, she feels there is not enough signage at the ground floor, indicating how to get to the hypermarket. The signage is not clear, the direction boards are not placed at eye level, and it is not easy to find the autowalk. In Far East countries where *seeing* is important, store managers often neglect this need for user friendly and easy-to-see direction boards.

> **Editor's note:**
> Throughout this book you will find references to trolleys, or what Americans would usually call a shopping cart. In Asia, many malls are built on multiple levels and customers can take their trolleys from one level to another via a moving walkway or a travelator.

## Hypermarket: the non-food floor

Suzy finds the autowalk and enters the hypermarket at the second floor. A store staff greets her; as a customer, she doesn't formally say hello in return, but as a polite person, she simply nods briefly. This staff-member at the entrance is here to show that the store cares about human contact, and to encourage shoppers to take a brochure about the promotions. Suzy already has her brochure that she received at home so she just takes a shopping cart. The trolley is not very dirty but there are pieces of paper and something that looks like a vegetable leaf; she doesn't mind too much about that. However, the trolley is a little squeaky and one of the wheels doesn't seem to roll very well. Like an astonishing 20 percent of the hypermarket shoppers in Asia, Suzy feels dissatisfied with the trolley because it runs badly. Suzy decides to leave this shopping cart and use another one.

She now has two routes to choose from. She can walk straight ahead, along the main promotion aisle with lots of special offers. Or, she can also turn to the right, and walk on the aisle that leads to the checkout counters. This way she could reach more quickly the packaged goods section, which she is mostly interested in, but she would bypass a large number of aisles and shelf space. Suzy opts for seeing the whole store and for checking out every aisle.

Shoppers in Asia do not always know which route to take in a store but generally want to be quite sure they have seen everything there is to see. Asian store managers think the same way. If shoppers do not see all the promotional podiums and all the shelf talkers, they're afraid the store will lose sales. They feel a store should not have too many entrances and exits, because shoppers might leave before going through all the aisles. Many Western store managers feel differently and believe it's okay if shoppers are not always exposed to everything in the store. They think some shoppers may also rather go quickly to the departments they need, like fresh food. For them the issue is not to force shoppers to go through all the aisles of the store, but to showcase strategic departments. Both may be right.

In the future, Asian shoppers will become more accustomed to modern trade, will become discerning enough to purchase what they want if they want it, and will value their time more than they do currently. In that respect, they will come to appreciate store chains that provide a quick, user-friendly pathway that facilitates their shopping as opposed to consuming too much of their time.

Suzy definitely wants to see the promotions at the main aisle. There are price tags marked with a felt pen in bright red color and slashed prices. By seeing all this, Suzy feels there are several bargains she cannot miss. For instance, there is an offer on electric fans. They are quite simple table fans and two are sold for the price of one; it looks really affordable. She decides to buy one set of two-for-one, and thinks she might give one to her parents because they need cooling equipment at their home.

The promotional aisle and the overall layout of the store are not unlike what shoppers in Europe or North America experience. The difference

in Asia lies in the way shoppers can see the displays and
the special offers. On average, Asians are shorter than
Westerners and a Korean or a Japanese housewife, in
particular, will actually be less at ease in a store if the shelves
are too high, simply because she will not be able to see the
store as a whole and will lose her sense of direction. In those

Editor's note:
Outside of the
U.S., merchandise
displays or shelves
may be referred to
as gondolas.

two countries, many department stores and general merchandise outlets
use gondolas that are shorter than in other countries. There is another
point however, about what shoppers see in a store; Asian shoppers need
guidance about direction. As they cannot always ask store employees
about directions, shoppers need good signage. While a Western shopper
may feel it's quite natural to walk in a sales area and find his or her way
quite leisurely, Asians will feel there is a "right way" to visit a store. One
can interpret this as being first-degree or a need to ensure they see 100
percent of the store. For this, Asian shoppers rely on direction signage.
They will express comments such as:

*"I'd like to have a store map showing all sections of the store."*

*"I had to walk in circles to arrive at the section that I want."*

*"The store signs are too high, I can't see them."*

*"I didn't even notice there is signage in the store."*

What is important during a customer's visit in store is very much about
signboards. Shoppers wish to know two things: "In what section am I?"
and "Is this a promotion?" So the department signage must be clear and
legible from the main aisle. A product display needs to highlight clearly
what kind of special offer is available, and has to be easy to read, written
in dark letters. Direction boards are important also because in Asia, the
shoppers don't spontaneously ask store employees about directions or
promotion details. To be fair, the employees do look very busy, as we've
mentioned, carrying products on palettes from the storage area to the
retail zone, refilling shelves, adjusting price tags, etc. They are supposed to
be in the store primarily to serve the customers but the employees are also

victims of seeing is believing. They are in store to work, and for them work has to be visible and quantifiable. You can quantify time, so if they work quickly and rapidly place all the products on a shelf, that's a measurable accomplishment. Physically putting the products on shelves and seeing the nice result with all the items stacked together is also something that you can appreciate visually. But talking to customers is not easily quantifiable; it doesn't feel like visible work. We also must say that store employees are not usually trained to believe that a shopper has priority.

The floor where Suzy entered sells what are called non-food items. Cultural products (books, CDs, and magazines sometimes), big and small appliances (TVs, DVD players, but also washing machines, refrigerators, iron, rice cookers, etc), clothing (usually some basic garments for the whole family) as well as hard goods like tools, simple ready-to-assemble furniture, cleaning equipment, and housewares. Suzy wants to have a look at the kitchen utensils and cooking pans. The woks look quite nice and big, but when she takes one in hand, it feels too lightweight and she prefers not to buy it. On the other hand, there are quite a few types of cooking bowls for microwave ovens, that are on promotion and she is interested.

When she reaches the toys section, Suzy is happy to be here with her little boy. A large, well-packaged radio controlled car is displayed and she feels it could be a nice toy for her five-year-old. She doesn't want him to be spoiled but in her mind, his childhood is almost over. For the next fifteen years or more, he is going to spend most of his time at school and will also study with tutors or at cram schools. In a way, now is his last period of being a child, so why not have a really nice gift for him. However, once inside the toy section she has a close look at the car. It doesn't look that large or that good any more. Suzy decides she will not take it. She also notices that the toy section seems bigger than last time with more choices but also more temptation and more risk of pester power. Suzy doesn't want to make her little boy unhappy or to have to say each time, "No, we can't buy this today." She feels some kind of resentment toward the store showcasing so many kinds of toys now, and trying to make her family buy too many playthings on impulse. Like many Asian mothers, she thinks that next time she is in this store with the family, maybe it would be best to avoid this section altogether. Next to the toys, there is a shelf space for writing instruments, dozens of pens and pencils in a multitude of colors. Some are very small size, about 3 inches; some are felt pens and markers. Quite a lot of kids, using the paper pads affixed on the shelves, are trying those pens and pencils. Suzy takes one or two.

## Apparel and accessories

A little further is the area for clothing near the autowalk. As the store has two levels, at some point shoppers use this travelator to go to the upper floor, dedicated to grocery and fresh food. Once they go to the upper floor and buy food items, it is unlikely that people like Suzy and her family would go back to the lower floor. So Suzy prefers to purchase all the non-food items she needs now, and only then move to the next floor.

At the clothing section, everything is presented on nice-looking fixtures. Even though all these clothes are basic, the merchandising is quite exciting. Because of all this, while looking around at the fixtures and touching the fabrics, Suzy wonders whether the prices are perhaps a bit higher than they should be. She also feels the designs look a bit too simple. She is not surprised by anything particularly new or trendy. Some of the outer garments and casual wear that she might like don't appear to be in store or she cannot find her size. After some thought, Suzy concludes that she didn't see any new arrivals today, and she moves on to the underwear department. In this store, the aisle for underwear is not near the checkout counters and Suzy is not going to feel embarrassed if she picks-up bras or looks at the selection of undergarments. The bags and accessories nearby also attract her. Some are based on cartoon characters and look cute. Suzy is more than thirty years old, but she might very well purchase a MinMie bag for her grocery shopping or a Minnie Mouse cap for outdoors so her face doesn't get too much sun. After deciding what she wants to buy, she goes with her son to the TV screen area to find her husband. He finally managed to park the car and called Suzy by cellphone to tell her he'd go to the home entertainment section. Then, they all go to the upper floor, to find groceries and fresh foods.

## Hypermarket: the food floor

Once at the food floor, which sells not only food, but also all kinds of packaged goods, including personal care and small cleaning items for the home, there are still lots of promotions to look at, and also lots of LCD screens showing various products. When those promotional screens first appeared in stores a few years before, Suzy used to think that the prices would be increased. If the store spends so much money displaying products on so much equipment, surely she has to pay for that in one way or another. Now she thinks differently. Those TV screens are paid for by the producers, not the hypermarket, and she thinks it's just part of the producers' advertising budget like the TV commercials or the newspaper print ads. And like some other Asian shoppers (slightly less than half, however), she does pay attention to these TV broadcasts in store.

On the food floor, the overall signage, or lack of, is quite important. For example, when Suzy arrives in front of a promotion of tissue paper, what she is looking at is a large display of a particular brand of tissue paper that is promoted. As the store did not indicate very clearly that this is just one specific offer, Suzy thinks this is the whole tissue category. If Suzy and many other Asian shoppers think this area is actually the whole tissue paper section and they don't see their usual brand, they will conclude the store doesn't have a very good selection and that it doesn't carry their preferred brand. It is unfortunate for the store because the other brands are in store, but they are displayed somewhere else. Suzy makes a point to look at all the aisles so eventually she will find what she is looking for, but will get the feeling that the product arrangement is not user-friendly because all the products of the same category were not in the same place. Other shoppers, if they don't check out every aisle, will perhaps miss the tissue paper section altogether.

In the meantime, Suzy's husband was looking for imported groceries.

He walked past the right section, but didn't find the products. Indeed, this imported food section is signed by a shelf space with flags from multiple countries. Suzy and her husband noticed the flags but they didn't automatically consider it means this is the section of imported foods. And they shouldn't. To them, a lot of colorful little flags of various countries looks nice, but does not clearly mean *imported packaged foods here*. Suzy and her family don't have a pet, but if they did, they might have a hard time with the pet section as well. The signage for that department shows some imagery of dogs and cats. These pictures are visible and well executed, but they don't state clearly what this is about. Shoppers in Asia need to read obvious mentions such as Pet Foods Section, or Pet Accessories on a banner to clearly understand that this area is about products for domesticated animals. Asian shoppers need clarity.

Suzy also wants to see the hygiene and beauty products that are located between the groceries and the fresh foods. She likes that area because it looks extra clean and the lighting is bright. The cosmetics, hair color and styling products are well-known, famous brands and the prices are reasonable. Suzy remembers that at first, when she started shopping at hypermarkets, she had a bad feeling about products for personal care in this kind of store. In some way, Suzy used to think that a store, even a big one, cannot sell large quantities of these packaged goods, so perhaps, some of the cosmetics would stay on the shelf for a long time, and she might buy an "old product." Hypermarkets are not specialists in beauty and cosmetics, so it was probably better for her to purchase all those at retailers that were purely focused on personal care. Being first-degree, Suzy just could not trust a hypermarket 100 percent when it came to beauty and hygiene. But this was a long time ago. Now, she not only skims through this area, but the health and beauty items represent about 10 percent of all what her family buys in this hypermarket.

Toward the end of their shopping visit, the family goes to the fresh food area. Like most shoppers in Asia, Suzy is not really fond of fresh produce at hypermarkets or supercenters. She prefers to buy at traditional markets that are closer to home, and where the produce is very fresh and less expensive. Her main reason to shop here today is for groceries and this will constitute more than 60 percent of her purchases. Fresh will represent just 10 percent or so, whereas in the West, the shoppers at hypermarkets allocate about 30 percent of their expenditure on fresh products.

She checks out the vegetables and the fish, by looking at the products, but she is not going to smell them. She also goes to the meat section. There seems to be a big promotion on beef. An employee just brought a meat display rack from the butcher department and lots of shoppers are gathered around it and around the meat cabinets. Suzy approaches. A dozen customers or more are standing by the chiller tables that contain pieces of beef loins and sirloins, for them to select on a self-serve basis. They are all manipulating with bare hands the pieces of meat they can grab, and they all look closely at each cut. Some put back the cuts they were examining and check another piece of loin, until one seems satisfactory and they place it in their trolleys. Suzy feels a bit disgusted. She is thinking that at least some of those people didn't wash their hands properly and feels that, even if she were to deep boil this meat, she wouldn't be sure about the germs. Finally, Suzy decides not to buy those sirloins. It's a pity she thinks; the price was good, but after all those hands touching the meat, she just doesn't feel like buying. Instead, she will purchase some pre-wrapped steaks and pork chops. She verifies that the pork has not been frozen because it then would have, as she puts it, a "taste of ice" that she doesn't like. Her perception has been evolving in the last few years though, as she starts to think that fresh pork bought at a modern store is not going to really taste different than what she buys at traditional trade. Besides she notes that there is no bad smell at the meat department here, unlike what she experiences at wet markets from time to time. She also buys chilled poultry: it is cheaper than fresh chicken and appears quite tender. She also thinks the taste is quite the same whether she buys chilled or fresh chicken.

A large facing of oranges a few meters away also attracts her. She is impressed by the big display; the bigger the better when seeing is believing.

The oranges look good; they are not too big, the skin has some lines on it, which means for Suzy that the fruit will be sweet, and the skin is also soft when you press it. And last but not least, the oranges are on promotion so she thinks they won't be more expensive than at wet markets. Suzy is definitely *sold*. The irony about this is that the other hypermarket not that far away is promoting the very same oranges, from same origin, and with the same quality. The other hypermarket is offering an even better price but their promotion is not as successful because their display is smaller. The space allocated to a promotion actually has an impact on the shoppers in Asia. If you see a special offer on a very large display, the promotion will be perceived better than a medium-size display, even if the medium display offers the same items at a price that's a little cheaper.

There are several kinds of fruits and vegetables in chiller cabinets that are pre-packed and Suzy wants to have a closer look. She notices that most of those claim to be organic foods and they have a "best before" date. Their prices are higher than for the other fruits and vegetables. Suzy has a doubt about those. She thinks that since they are pre-packed they may have been stored in a refrigerator for a long time or perhaps frozen, and they might become rotten. She is also not convinced that organic produce offers more nutrition or is better for health, even when it is not sold in chiller cabinets.

Generally speaking Suzy prefers to buy traditional fruits and vegetables that are on the counter and that were not refrigerated. For her, and for a majority of shoppers in Asia, really fresh produce is displayed loose on a counter. She feels that fresh foods don't stay overnight on a counter. She likes to check the freshness mostly from the appearance. Her criteria are that the produce should have a bright color, should be not too soft, and should look juicy, not dry. In Suzy's view, a vegetable with leaves that are yellowish, for instance, will be harmful to health. Checking visually is far more important to her than posters about safety assurance or traceability. As a matter of fact, she doesn't notice these types of signage about safety and even if she paid attention, she wouldn't know if this is real information and would not consider this factor. For her there is no way to prove if it is true.

At home, Suzy received a brochure that showcased all the nice promotions the hypermarket offers. She noticed some good deals about a new shampoo. Suzy did not buy the shampoo today, for a simple reason: She didn't find it. It was not at the beauty section and the promotional display was not on her path. The shampoo has nice looking signage but it is located along the autowalk that links both floors of the hypermarket. In order to really notice the promotional podium of this shampoo, shoppers like Suzy would have to make a U-turn when they alight from the autowalk. However shoppers tend to continue walking straight ahead; they do not anticipate that a potentially interesting offer might lie just alongside the travelator, which is now behind them. Although Suzy usually doesn't talk with the staff, this time she asked about this shampoo promotion. The problem is, the staff member didn't know. Although this was a major promotional effort, supported by a print ad and brochures, the logistics were not quite right. The product was not well situated and the staff had not been briefed.

Asian shoppers stay on average about 50 to 55 minutes at a hypermarket, not counting the time spent in the parking lot or the shopping gallery on the ground floor, or at the food court. As we have seen, they may be confused and lost, and they may not purchase all the things they wanted. At the end Suzy probably did not buy all she planned to, even though the products were there and the prices were right. When we conduct exit surveys, we often identify a large number of products the shoppers say they wanted to buy but could not find. However, about half of those "not found items" are actually sold by the store. They are not out of stock, but the customers simply did not see them.

Incidentally, shoppers who come to hypermarkets may end up buying nothing at all. In Asian hypermarkets, 3 to 6 percent of the visitors usually exit without making a purchase. The share can sometimes amount to 10 percent, when the hypermarket is visited also to kill time and not really for shopping. In Asia this happens mostly in emerging countries.

## Checking out

For Suzy, the last stage before leaving the store is to go through the check-out counters. In Asia about 65 to 70 percent of shoppers at hypermarkets are relatively satisfied with the speed at checkout counters. About cashier friendliness the perception is much worse. It varies by country, but it is rare to find more than half of the shoppers in Asia being happy with the hospitality and friendliness of cashiers.

In the case of Suzy, she has noticed that even on Sunday afternoons, when so many people shop, the speed at checkout counters is not that bad. She sees that virtually all the checkout counters are open, so her conclusion is the store is doing its best to speed up service. For Suzy the issue is not so much about efficiency on weekends; it is more about weekday evenings, especially if she comes here after 7 or 8 p.m. That's the time when the store still has a sizeable number of shoppers and not many cashiers are at work. But all in all, she feels the quickness is acceptable.

About the friendliness of cashiers, Suzy would agree that this could be better. Unlike the West where one may feel that the only place where people are friendly is the checkout counter, because of store policies to smile and greet customers, cashiers' friendliness in Asia is seldom satisfactory. This has to do with expectations. Asian people anticipate that they will experience politeness and a friendly attitude, but this is hard to deliver for cashiers who feel overworked and underpaid. When we do in-store surveys in Asia, we often note a consistent decrease in satisfaction about friendliness at checkout counters as the day progresses.

Quite consistently, shoppers are more satisfied about the kindness of cashiers in the early morning, and much less toward the end of the day. If a store shows an average 40 percent satisfaction with cashiers' friendliness, it will exceed 45 to 50 percent before noon, and will decrease all the way below 30 percent satisfaction around 9 p.m.

After a long day, both the shoppers and cashiers are tired. It would make sense for a store to have a well-rested team of cashiers after 7 or 8 in the evening, but the issue of friendliness is not only about cashiers; it concerns all store employees. When Asian shoppers like Suzy buy fish, roast chicken, or fresh produce that needs to be weighed, the interaction with the store staff also shows a dichotomy. The speed and efficiency are perceived as very good (usually more than 90 percent satisfaction), whereas the friendliness and kindness are not (often much less than 50 percent satisfaction).

Once Suzy and her family have paid for what they bought, they don't have free plastic bags from the checkout counter. They used to, but now it's necessary for customers to bring their own rucksacks. Suzy has been told this is to protect the environment but she doesn't feel that she is playing a role in favor of ecology by bringing her own environmental bag, as it's called. She only thinks that it is an inconvenience and that she has to comply. When all the goods are packed they decide to go back home directly this time. They won't have an ice cream at the food court and won't buy shoes or accessories at the shopping gallery. Today, they don't plan to visit the store one floor up selling furniture and home improvements either. But once in a while, every four or five shopping visits at this mall, they also go there, at least to get new ideas about how to revamp and decorate their home or to check the prices of pieces of furniture. Actually most of the visitors at many category killers for home interior are browsers. Slightly more than 50 percent of the individuals who buy something in such outlets are converted browsers. Originally they just came to the store to look around. This is not counting the visitors who had an actual purchase intention, but finally exited the store because they didn't find anything to their liking: it is the case almost one third of the time.

For now, Suzy and her family simply go with their shopping cart to the travelator and then all the way to the parking lot in the basement. They are not in a hurry. As shoppers, parking is free for them for a couple of hours and it feels safe and clean. Suzy's husband remembers exactly where the car is parked; it's easy to remember because it is coded by letters and by colors. The only thing they don't like about the parking facility is that it is too small and not easy to get in or out. If they have difficulty exiting, they will perhaps have another look at the other hypermarket nearby in the near future.

# 4

# What Location Means in Asian Markets

THERE IS the same joke among professional retailers whether you are in Europe, the U.S., or the Far East. When retailers talk about what really matters if you want a store to be successful, they say, "There are three important things that are crucial; the first is location, the second is location, and the third is location." No matter how many times you hear this, it isn't very enlightening.

Over the years, our consultancy in Asia has been commissioned to judge hundreds of potential sites for retailers. Since retail chains invest several million dollars when opening new stores, it definitely makes sense for them to analyze in detail whether a location is good or not. What we do in this respect is visit the site, appraise the location based on specific criteria, perform a statistic treatment and ultimately, we forecast the sales potential. We tell the retailer how much sales the store will achieve.

To do this, we have determined a certain number of variables that relate to geographic location. In a nutshell, they are: visibility, accessibility, catchment area, competition, and cannibalization. Other things count as well, like the format or the image of the store chain, but these do not refer to location. In order to simplify, we will take hypermarkets as a general example, but when relevant, will address other formats.

## Visibility

Since "seeing is believing" is a major notion in Asia, let's examine how this applies to a store location. Visibility will determine whether a store will be easy to notice or not. This is true both in the case of large outlets like department stores and hypermarkets or small shops like a mini-mart or a convenience store.

A small-size outlet such as a convenience store or a family-run store (also known as a mom-and-pop shop) needs, as much as a big-box outlet, to be strongly visible. There are four sub-criteria about visibility:

- **Is the site open or closed?** A site is *open* when there is no particular obstacle blocking the view when you are in the immediate surroundings. Conversely a site is *closed* when, due to other buildings or trees or an excess of advertising billboards or any other obstacle, you might pass near the store and not see it. In large Asian urban centers, there are not many open sites any more, but in markets like secondary cities in China or some parts of Indonesia, Vietnam, or even Thailand up-country, many open sites are still available.

- **Is the site located directly at the junction of two roads?** If yes, its visibility is strengthened significantly.

- **Is there sufficient frontage for the store?** Unless the show window or the whole frontage is poorly maintained, the wider the better. In developing markets, but also in secondary cities of the developed markets like Korea or Taiwan, the show windows sometimes do not look very good and become counter productive. However, generally speaking, a large frontage will make the store more noticeable and this is a good thing. The important point here is not just the width. A hypermarket, for example, can have a frontage of 300 meters but if it is not directly on the sidewalk of the street, the overall visibility will be weak. When big-box stores are part of a shopping mall they often suffer from a real lack of visibility if they are in the basement or if the signage in the mall is not user-friendly. They may be large stores, with large frontage but in effect they do not benefit from an open site.

- **How big is the road?** A wide avenue offers better visibility, obviously, but this is mitigated by the open/closed notion: even a six- or eight-lane avenue cannot provide great visibility if the store is partly hidden by a gasoline station, as sometimes happens in emerging countries.

All in all, the notion of visibility is not a fundamental parameter in Asia because once a store is open, people in the area will know about it and they will not worry too much about whether or not it is easy to see. Access on the other hand is one of the most crucial parameters.

## Accessibility

It is relatively simple to gauge the accessibility of a store. We first evaluate what we call the natural access. In a country like China where shoppers travel mostly by bus, we have to consider how easy or difficult it will be to reach the store from all directions by bus. In a market like Vietnam, Cambodia, or even Taiwan, where huge numbers of people travel by motorcycle, we appraise the accessibility by motorbikes. And in countries where shoppers travel mostly by car like Thailand and Korea, we will consider how easy or difficult it is to access the store by car, from north, east, south, and west.

To measure this, we go on location and experience the accessibility in real life. For example, we drive to the site from the north, then from the east, west, etc. When relevant we identify the number of bus stops, the possibility or not to do a U-turn by car and motorbike, or the presence of subway stations within walking distance. Depending on the store category, the means of transport are more or less critical. A subway station will be important in the case of department stores or supermarkets, but will be almost negligible for the hypermarkets. On the other hand, accessibility by car may be a major issue for a hypermarket, but will not matter for a convenience store or a small personal care retail outlet.

The natural accessibility can be weak but it is sometimes partly compensated by other means of access. For instance, in some Asian countries, emerging markets mostly, big stores organize systems of shuttle buses to bring customers to and from areas where they live. However, this does not make the location better; it is simply a way to counteract a location problem. It is also costly for a store to manage a shuttle bus system and not always efficient, since passengers can take advantage of the free transportation to the hypermarket downtown, while having no intention to actually shop there.

In addition to reaching the store from the four compass points, the accessibility parameters relate to traffic, the question being whether the road is a main thoroughfare. We found that in all Asian towns, large or small, if a big-box store is situated on one of the major roads, its attractiveness is reinforced. If the store is on a far-reaching axis, it will catch more shoppers than usual. So if a hypermarket in Seoul should normally capture shoppers up to 18 to 20 minutes driving distance by car away in all directions, it would attract customers as far as 24 to 26 minutes by car along the far-reaching road. The difference does not appear extreme; we are still talking about 20 minutes or so, but theoretically 5 additional minutes may involve a catchment area that is more than 50 percent larger. This does not necessarily translate into 50 percent more customers, but it makes a difference.

Another question is the traffic fluidity in the area. Again in our Seoul example, if driving 20 minutes takes you four kilometers away or six kilometers away, the total area where you catch customers regroups very different population levels. However, for most developed countries in Asia, we should not over-estimate this difference, because if the traffic is particularly fluid, it is a bonus for a big store but this bonus amounts to 5 to 7 percent more potential customers. Traffic fluidity will not magically increase the potential by half. This issue of fluid traffic is relevant for large stores only. We have not identified anything significant about this in cases of small outlets such as a convenience stores or a small supermarket. It would mean walking more or less quickly on the sidewalk on the way to the convenient store, the supermarket, or to a coffee shop. In theory the sidewalks can be more or less crowded and therefore show a difference on walking speed, but in practical terms, in all the cities and towns that we studied in Asia, we could not determine an equivalent to traffic fluidity for small outlets when shoppers usually come on foot.

There are still other sub-criteria on accessibility such as whether the site of the store is on a slope—which often happens in China, whether entering the parking lot will be easy, whether the area in general is already a major commercial destination or not.

A slope has a relatively weak impact, but the issue of parking entrance is important especially if a U-turn is involved. An Asian customer may accept driving an extra 800 meters to make a U-turn, if it's **on his way back home**. In other words, when he drives from home, he accesses the store easily; the extra 800 meters for the U-turn happens only when he returns. Conversely if the U-turn is on the way to the store, the Asian customer feels increasingly (more so in 2011 than in 2001) that he is wasting too much of his time because he still has to do all the shopping and will have to return home in addition. However, in both cases the extra 800 meters essentially involve the same length of time.

There are also criteria about access that relate to superstitions or *feng shui*, if you pass by a specific location or if the store is situated at a place that has special meaning. These are not rational considerations, but have an impact because shoppers will decide not to come to the store even though technically, it's easy to access. In China for instance, there were many battles during the occupation by the Japanese and also during the confrontations between the military forces of Mao Tse Tung and of Chiang Kai-shek in the 1940s. Some battles took place in cities, and the parts of towns where many fighters or civilians were killed are considered haunted by some people. Most retailers dare not open stores in these areas because they feel that customers will be afraid of ghosts and will hesitate to shop there.

Other sites may be considered as bringing bad luck as well. In some cases, *feng shui* masters are often persuaded to officially approve a "bad-omen location" in exchange for a symbolic token, such as the construction of a small pond nearby (water and carp will bring good luck) or something that reflects light (mirrors or metallic façades) because this will also repulse bad spirits. If a bridge or a special walkway needs to be constructed, the investment may even involve hundreds of thousands of dollars. The feng shui master makes some money and the location is now auspicious so shoppers will come. In some other cases, not only in China, if a feng shui expert says the site is bad omen, it happens that the retailer gives up on the project and doesn't develop the piece of land for retail, even if, from a logical standpoint, it is prime real estate. However, this reflects more on the Asian businessmen's way of thinking than on shoppers' behavior.

Among all sub-criteria regarding access, the really important one is the one we call natural access; the secondary one being traffic fluidity, in the case of large outlets. For small stores the natural access and the presence of public transport such as a subway station or bus stops in the vicinity are the major sub-criteria.

However, even more important than the accessibility is the total zone where the store will operate. This zone is called the catchment area, because it is the territory where the store will catch, or capture, potential customers. It is also known as trading zone or store zone.

## Catchment area

The number of residents, their wealth, and their expenditure levels, and the population concentration of the total geographic area where a store operates all have an impact on the ultimate success or failure of a store. These all relate to the catchment area.

Population levels, usually considered in terms of households, is a crucial factor in selecting a retail location, but this is not the only key to success. Here too, we have to consider several sub-points such as the population density, especially in the proximity zones.

All else being equal, Store A in a territory of 100,000 households may be in better position than Store B in a catchment area of 150,000 resident households, if the bulk of the population is concentrated in proximity for Store A. We define proximity, in the case of hypermarkets, category killers, and department stores, as five minutes driving time. In Asia the overall catchment area corresponds to about 20 minutes driving distance. Technically this means that more than 80 percent of store sales turnover comes from customers who shop regularly and reside less than 20 minutes away. There are a few customers who live beyond that distance and, for whichever reason, shop the store regularly but they are scattered, not grouped in a specific sub-zone. We address these out-of-zone customers at the end of the section about competitive environment.

In Asia, we identified a rule of thumb that we call internally the retail 80–20 rule. It has nothing to do with the Pareto Principle. Our rule simply says, in general, that for a large store (not a supermarket nor a small convenience store), people who live within 20 minutes driving time will generate 80 percent of sales. In some cases a store may even have a larger catchment area. For instance, a flagship store will attract residents in a whole city. In the countryside, if there are few shopping destinations, a large store can have a 45-minute catchment area. However, generally speaking, in Asia a store zone for a category killer, a hypermarket, or a department store, is about 20 minutes.

Once we know that, we still have to consider the catchment with some detail. Someone living 18 minutes away will be much less likely to shop the store than a same-age, same-income resident living 2 minutes away. Therefore we need to separate the catchment into three isochronous subzones, which are:

- within 5 minutes distance,
- between 6 and 10 minutes, and
- between 11 and 20 minutes.

Those are generally called primary zone, secondary zone, and tertiary zone, and usually the words proximity and primary zone have the same meaning.

In a market where most shoppers come by bus, such as many cities in China, we consider minutes as traveling time by bus, and if people use cars like in Seoul, Korea, we calculate based on driving distance by car, etc.

Checking the driving distance by bus, car or motorcycle is easy. We simply have to follow a bus for instance, during various hours of the day, ideally both during weekend and weekdays. However, evaluating population density is not so easy because in many Asian countries, population statistics are not accurate enough. Official data exist and will tell you how many families are registered in a certain district of a certain city, but unfortunately these statistics often are wrong. They may be outdated and even if they are recent, the data only tell you about the people or the households officially registered. In real life, in the countries where retail chains expand aggressively such as China, Thailand, and Indonesia as well as other developing markets, many big cities actually host a large number of people who are not registered there. They are still registered in their hometown but not in the bigger city where they live in order to work. Here we are not simply referring to unskilled migrant workers who come to town to find a job during non-farming seasons, we are mainly referring to qualified and white collar workers who move from one town to another, but don't feel the necessity to be registered with the statistic bureau. These residents live, work, and purchase goods and services in town but they don't appear in the official data.

So, the national statistics may tell you there are 100,000 households residing in a territory whereas, in reality, there could be an extra 30,000 living and consuming there or it could be the other way round. To address this issue and find more accurate population levels, we need to approach local authorities at the sub-district or street level. They know how many people and families live in their streets. Doing this is time consuming, however. When we interview residents at any given location, we also systematically ask if they are registered at the place where they live, or whether they are still registered elsewhere. Retailers often forget about these non-registered populations, although it is a critical issue. Roughly speaking in large Asian cities for markets other than Japan, Korea, Hong Kong or Singapore, we may have between 10 to 25 percent more middle-class residents than the statistics say. Again, these people are not migrant workers with low purchasing power but are actual shoppers usually coming from mid-size towns in the country.

The population density in proximity versus the rest of the catchment area is important but so is the apparent wealth of the residents. Roughly speaking, in the more developed Asian markets (Korea, Japan, Hong Kong, Taiwan, Singapore but also Malaysia and Thailand) virtually all the population has enough income to go to department stores and hypermarkets. But in less developed countries like Indonesia, the Philippines, Vietnam, Cambodia, Laos, or parts of China, there is a proportion (between 10 to 35 percent of residents) who do not have enough income to shop at modern trade in the first place. Since in most Asian countries the local statistics are not sufficiently accurate about incomes and consumption patterns, we perform a quantitative study and randomly interview the residents about their household and personal incomes, their detailed expenditure levels by product categories, and their purchase likelihood if a particular format were to open.

Another element about catchment areas, which is also underestimated quite often, has to do with what we call "barriers." We studied cases in several countries for store projects with high population density, both in the proximity zones and in the overall catchment area, and also with lifestyles that are reasonably high. All this sounds extremely positive. However, the population centers might be separated or blocked from the store location by physical barriers—obstacles that in some way are going to hamper the visit to a store. A barrier can be a river even though a bridge is constructed, or a railroad or even a highway even though it is possible to cross those. On paper, the catchment area may seem nice in terms of density, wealth, visibility, and access (after all if there is a bridge you can cross the river or the railroad).

Beijing is a typical example of this. It is a traditional Chinese city, organized with large avenues extending north-south and east-west, with, at its center, the imperial palace, the Forbidden City. The avenues are wide and there are half a dozen ring roads circling the city, which are easy to see on any city map. In Beijing, a large store is generally easy to access, including by public transports like the bus system. A store can therefore be very accessible, visible, located in a part of the city where residents have the purchasing power, and with a dense population. However such a store with apparently a wonderful location will not attract residents who live beyond "the next ring-road," even if they live only 6 or 7 minutes away including the time to cross this ring road. Customers simply don't plan to cross and will shop another store if there is one.

Some barriers may also be psychological and not physical in nature. Even then, a large ratio of Asian customers will be reluctant to come. Psychological barriers for instance, can be administrative. In the Taiwanese city of Kaohsiung a category killer may have a store in the northern part of town in the district called Nanzih and the management would name its outlet after the district: Nanzih Store. In this case the problem would be that many target customers living just 7 or 8 minutes away would not shop there, for reasons in large part psychological and first-degree. Because they live in Zuoying district, for example, they will feel that if the store is in another district, it is probably cumbersome to go all the way. Seeing is believing: If the name tells you it's another district, it can be interpreted as being "not for me." It is better to give the store a neutral name like Lotus Flower Store, than to name it after the district, which may create a psychological barrier.

A last point about catchment area and population density relates to relocation trends. In all cities, some districts grow less residential over time while others show rapid population growth. As we've mentioned in Chapter 1, this can be due to local government policies, but it can also stem from a real estate developer who invests in a part of the city and builds a large housing complex. There are quite a few real estate developers in any given city, and many residential building programs may be implemented.

Over the course of ten or fifteen years, these developments will host several thousand households, with targeted profiles and income brackets. When a store opens at a specific location with the plan to stay in operation there for a few decades, management needs to evaluate these long term trends. If, for instance, 8,000 households are going to live in a residential complex in proximity and half of them relocate from the city center (the other half may come from various other areas), then it means an additional 8,000 resident households will live in the primary zone. It also means there will be 4,000 fewer customer households downtown — which may be the primary zone for another store of the same retail chain. The good news is that all this can be reasonably quantified and retailers can integrate these demographic trends in their expansion strategies.

## Gravity Laws

A chapter about store location could not be complete without referring to the researchers William J. Reilly and David L. Huff.

In the late 1920s, Reilly was inspired by astronomy and the laws of gravity that command stars and planets (*The Law of Retail Gravitation*, Pilsbury Publishers, 1972). He worked on business interactions between cities and concluded that the transactions depend on the distance between cities and their respective size, in the same way as the law of gravitation works. In the 1960s, Huff hypothesized that if, at a given place, customers have the choice between only two shopping destinations, A and B, there is a certain probability for them to go to A, and another probability for them to shop at B. All else being equal, the probability stems from the respective size of A and B and their distance from the place where the customers are. If the two stores have the same net sales area and are equally distant from the customers they will each have a 50 percent probability of attracting any given customer. The formulae are relatively easy to find with academic sources or via the internet. Simply put, they say that a store's capacity to attract shoppers will increase or decrease according to the square of the distance. If residents live one kilometer away from a store, they will be nine times more likely to shop there than if they live three kilometers away; not just three times more likely. As for the size of two stores, or net sales area, the calculation is a little more complex but roughly speaking, when two stores are equidistant, if one is significantly larger than the other, it's attractiveness will be around 25 percent higher (this also depends on the products sold).

Many retail professionals worldwide have heard of these laws, under the name Huff Model or, most of the time, Gravity Model. They more or less know that a store will attract shoppers in the same way as a celestial body such as a star will attract satellites or planets. This is related to human science however, so the phrase "all else being equal" is key. In the retail world, we never have similar roads and traffic conditions, the same visibility or a homogenous population density for two stores with no barriers at all. Very often, there are even more than two competitors situated within a catchment area, which makes the judgment about location more complex.

## Competitive environment

Since we mention competitors, let's recognize that the "location, location, location" statement doesn't really tell you much about competitive stores. Is it always bad to have a competitor nearby or does it reinforce the attractiveness of the area? And how do we define competitive stores?

Simply put, a competitor is not always what professional retailers will say it is, but it is always what shoppers experience. For example, a director of a supermarket may think that, strategically, his competitors are other supermarkets, but in fact a majority of his Asian customers also shop for food at wet markets and hypermarkets. A hypermarket director believes a cash-and-carry outlet or a member club is a different concept than his store, but his shoppers go to both the hypermarket and the cash-and-carry when they want discount grocery items. A mid-scale department store will officially compete with other department stores but in real life in Asia, it also competes with the upscale hypermarket when there is one in the catchment area. A convenience store competes with other such stores, but also with the small family-run shops that are present in most cities of Asia, and also with supermarkets and hypermarkets.

Competitors are not only the stores having the same format and offering the same concept. A competitor's impact depends on many things: the assortment offered, price points and promotion policies, employees' dedication, and the various services provided. We address commercial offers in the coming chapters. But primarily, competition depends on geography.

Geographically, we first have to differentiate whether competitors are located in the primary zone or in the zones beyond. This is simple. Let's take hypermarket A that has two competitors—hypermarkets with a similar image and similar sales area. If one competitor is located five minutes away from hypermarket A and the other one is fifteen minutes away, the competitive impact will be very different. If all else is equal, the competitor, which is five minutes distance, is going to jeopardize hypermarket A about nine times more than the hypermarket located a quarter of an hour away. In other words, a store surrounded by seven or eight competitors located 15 minutes away could be better off than if there is just one competitor situated next door.

This may sound surprising. If you look at a map and see that a store is completely surrounded by seven or eight others, you might feel its situation is more hopeless than if it has only one competitor, even in proximity. But this is what often happens and it is described by the Gravity Law as the attractiveness is proportional to the square of the distance.

There are two other points about competition other than Gravity Laws and distance among competitors. One is what we call the vulnerability of a store's site. Here again, many things could look good in terms of overall location: good visibility, easy access, no barriers, a population that is dense with appropriate levels of wealth and not too many competitors. Most retail chains would probably want to open a store right away in such a location, but you need to validate whether the site is vulnerable.

The question to ask is, what happens if a competitor comes in after you just opened your store? This is a valid question because in Asia there are ways for retailers to open stores at various places including very near each other. A competitor can always appear next to your store.

Will your existing store lose half of the daily sales turnover overnight? If both stores have the same size, same image, and the same offer, and are almost at the same location, they basically share the same trading zone, a similar accessibility and visibility, and will face the same problems of barriers if there are some.

What will happen relates to the issue of by-pass. If your store is accessible essentially from a road going north-south and the new competitor opens just 200 meters north, this competitor will jeopardize a large part of the north of your catchment area. Shoppers coming from the north are likely to stop at the competition's store first, and miss yours. If there is just one road leading to your site, you run a serious risk. Conversely if your site is at a crossroads, the chances are that your store will remain accessible for most shoppers, at least for the ones coming from east, west, and south, and they will see you first. So your store is much more vulnerable if it's located on a single road, like the north-south axis above, versus being at a crossroad.

Then you still need to analyze the population density in all the catchment area. In our example, if the population centers are concentrated toward the north, your store is much more vulnerable than if the population density is equally spread within the store zone. In one case, not only are you in danger of losing the northern part of your catchment area, but also this part is the most promising due to population potentials. In the other case the risk is less acute.

In Asia, the issue of site vulnerability is not too severe in small or medium-sized towns, especially in developing countries. This is because the infrastructure in those towns will be developing, and usually more and better roads are being built, because the population is growing. Large cities in Asia represent more risks of vulnerability because the population is not growing as fast, including for middle class households. The suburbs of large cities are the zones showing population growth. City dwellers move out of downtown and go to suburbs and medium-size satellite cities around the large megapolis. In Shanghai, Seoul, Bangkok, Jakarta, and Tokyo, among others, partly because of cost and because of local authorities, the increase in population within the large cities is slow or even negative, whereas more and more residents move out toward neighboring towns. With this background in mind, a store can open in those suburbs or satellite cities and expect the road systems to improve and see the population potential grow significantly, thus reducing vulnerability.

Our last point about competitors and location is what we can call a synergy effect: when several competitors, such as food retailers or hypermarkets, open their stores in the same catchment area, not too distant from one another. We see this in many Asian markets and intuitively, you may think those will compete intensely and none of these stores might be profitable. The opposite can be true, because Asian shoppers will expect interesting offers in that area, since four stores have more to offer than just one outlet. The customers will be cherry picking, certainly, but on the other hand these 3 or 4 outlets will constitute a strong shopping destination and they will attract far beyond the usual 20 minutes. Shoppers will perhaps visit one store today and on the way back home, stop at another to see what's new. Two weeks later they will shop at the third store and check out the last one as well.

Some customers do this partly to find a great bargain but also because it's considered fun: reviewing the assortments and the promotions is a way to save a bit of money, but it is leisure too. Even at a hypermarket, shopping is not perceived as mundane as in the West; to some people it is almost a hobby. In Asia, shopping is actually one of the main activities for an average household, sometimes the third-ranked activity on weekends, after general care of the home and kids, and watching TV. In many markets in the region, shopping is a type of leisure that is comparable to a family picnic or an afternoon at the cinema in the West. Depending on countries and urbanization levels, other than watching TV or taking care of the home, weekend activities are much more related to shopping (between 55 and 70 percent of the middle class respondents we interviewed) than related to cinema for instance (less than 10 percent).

Shopping is also a leisure activity in the case of category killers. An area with three or more stores for home decorating for example will become the primary destination for shoppers who want to see furniture or do-it-yourself products. Although the proximity zone will seem to be saturated, the stores may very well thrive because they attract a large number of out-of-zone customers who live beyond the catchment area.

A typical hypermarket (i.e., not in synergy with others to extend its catchment) will generate about 12 to 15 percent of its sales from these out-of-zone shoppers. The same is true for a category killer or a department store in Asia, so the out-of-zone shoppers cannot be ignored. Customers who drive, say, 30 minutes to go to a store know that the shopping trip consumes time so they'll buy more than the average shoppers. Their average shopping basket can be a little higher than those of customers who live in first, second, or tertiary zones. Large stores, since they display a wide or a deep selection tend to attract these out-of-zone shoppers because the customers know they have a good chance of finding the assortment they want and potentially great promotions with a single shopping trip. Other than out-of-zone, we must mention the occasional shoppers who usually represent 5 to 6 percent of the sales of a large store. They may visit less than once a month, less than once a quarter, or just once a year depending on the type of store and the way marketing people decide to define occasional (as opposed to regular) customers.

## Cannibalization

While the competitive background is significant when we analyze the importance of location, thanks to the synergy effect, it is not always as negative as you may think. Another form of competition is when two outlets from the same retail brand operate in the same catchment area or share part of the same trading zone.

This issue, when a store is competing with another branch of the same retail chain, is called cannibalization. It actually happens often in Asia and retailers are always concerned about the outcome. Often, cannibalization happens when a chain takes over another one. In many countries, you can find two retailers from the same brand located within a few hundred meters of each other because the company acquired another retail chain and converted the stores. However, cannibalization is mitigated if a physical or psychological barrier separates the two stores. Cannibalization is sometimes defensive or strategic. That occurs when a retail chain does not want a store to be overcrowded and is concerned that service quality is deteriorating. It is also when a chain does not want to see new competitors coming to its catchment area.

When Tesco wanted to enter Taiwan in 2000, Carrefour was, and remains, the leader among hypermarkets. To prevent Tesco from expanding profitably, Carrefour opted for a saturation approach. The city of Taoyuan, south of Taipei, illustrates this strategy. In Taoyuan, Carrefour already had three stores when it learned that Tesco was planning to build a hypermarket in that town. Knowing where the Tesco branch would open, Carrefour decided to build yet another branch nearby. The idea was that Carrefour stores would be present in the whole catchment area of the new Tesco hyper, both in proximity and tertiary zones so as to also pre-empt the out-of-zone potentials. By doing this, Carrefour would capture most of the market and avert a Tesco success story in the country. Carrefour stores were competing against each other as well but the company accepted cannibalization because the possible outcome was worth the risk. They were right. In that country, for a number of reasons, Tesco never became successful and five years after opening, the Tesco stores network in Taiwan was taken over by Carrefour.

The other reason for a retail brand to accept cannibalization is the one we mentioned earlier—when a store is too successful and is becoming more and more crowded over time, both on weekdays and weekends. If the shopping experience is not a good one for the retail brand's customers, the chain may want to transfer some of the shoppers from the original store to a new one, sharing part of the same catchment area, instead of waiting and seeing the current customers desert the original store little by little, because they no longer appreciate the shopping environment.

## The real three challenges

In fact, the challenge for a store cannot just be summed up by saying, "There are three criteria: location, location, location." Selecting a site is only one element, and we hope the pages above shed light on what location actually involves.

The operational key to success starts once the retail outlet is constructed and you can no longer change the place. At that time, the retailer has to address three additional challenges. They are penetration rate, shopping frequency, and average ticket.

Penetration rate refers to the proportion of resident households who are your customers. If a store operates in a catchment area of 100,000 households and if 25,000 households are customers, the store has 25 percent penetration rate. As we have seen, a large store can usually capture customers within 20 minutes driving distance or so. Therefore it is relatively easy to identify the number of households living in the catchment area and, once the store is open, to determine how many of these resident households have actually become customers.

Frequency of shopping is generally calculated by weeks. If a given customer shops exactly once per week at the store, her frequency of shopping is 1; if she only shops once every fortnight, the shopping frequency is 0.5, and if she visits exactly once a day and buys something at each visit, her shopping frequency is 7, as stores are open seven days a week in Asian markets. Frequency of shopping works for department stores and food retailers because it is a habit to go there quite regularly.

However, we can also calculate the number of "yearly shopping visits" instead of weekly, mostly for category killers that sell products for home needs, because one doesn't buy appliances or furniture, or even toys every week. Customers who buy home interior products actually operate by projects. When they have some home renovation in mind for instance, they will go to a furniture store or a DIY outlet three or four times during the same month in order to purchase what they need to revamp the living room or the bathroom, because one shopping visit is not likely to be enough. And they may not visit at all for the rest of the year, so it does not make sense to consider a weekly frequency of shopping in those cases.

A basket or ticket refers to the amount spent during one shopping visit. If a customer spends $10, the basket is therefore ten dollars. Some of these calculations are tricky and may even be counter intuitive so we provide some details on this (see *Being careful with numbers*, below).

In any case, once a store is operating, those are the three and only three conditions that will determine the success or failure. A store needs to capture customers, to encourage them to visit often, and to grow their purchase amount when they shop. To achieve this, store management can leverage price, promotions, assortment, and services. Those are the commercial operations we address in the coming chapters.

# Being careful with numbers

For retailers, there is an easy method to gauge a marketing agency's knowledge of the retail business. This method works in every country and, we think, is simple enough. The retailer just needs to ask the agency, "What is the average frequency of shopping?" in a given situation.

The situation is this. Suppose we do an exit survey and interview shoppers after they bought something in the store. Among the things we ask, is the question, "How frequently do you shop this store?"

For simplicity let's consider the interviews are conducted perfectly, it is fully representative, there is no bias, it is conducted during a full week, and all the customers tell the truth. So if, for instance, Tuesday morning corresponds to exactly 4 percent of the weekly transactions of the actual store, then exactly 4 percent of the interviews will be done on Tuesday morning, etc. And, still for simplicity, let's say we have exactly 1,000 respondents and that half give the answer, "I shop this store exactly once a day" (i.e., 7 times a week) and the other 500 respondents give the answer, "I shop this store exactly once a week."

If you have to tell the retailer what the average shopping frequency is, the answer appears to be easy. Half visit once per week and half visit seven times. Therefore the average has to be four. However, if someone tells the retailer that customers average four shopping visits per week, the answer is wrong.

Why?

Let's imagine this store is a hypermarket that has 70,000 transactions in a typical week. If half of the transactions come from people shopping exactly once per week, then you need exactly 35,000 shoppers to achieve these 35,000 weekly transactions. Now, the other 35,000 transactions come from customers who shop seven times a week. How many shoppers are needed to generate 35,000 transactions in this case? Five thousand. Those 5,000 customers will come seven times, so in a week they will produce 35,000 tickets.

So in order to have 70,000 transactions the store actually had 40,000 customers in the week, the 35,000 weekly ones plus the 5,000 daily customers. The average frequency of shopping in that store is therefore $70,000 / 40,000 = 1.75$.

There is a large difference between 1.75 and 4. In our example the error is about frequency of shopping, but other mistakes can be made about penetration rates.

If a retail chain is given information that is wrong, such as a number that is more than twice the reality, both the retailer and the marketing agency run a risk. The retailer will implement marketing tactics based on the information and, even if those are well executed, it is likely that results will not meet expectations. The retailer may then insist and try harder, but eventually will waste time and energy fighting battles that can't be won. The agency will establish and propagate a rule of thumb that is wrong and this will damage the agency's reputation.

# 5

# A Nice Price Is Not Enough

A TYPICAL cliché about Asian customers is that they are purely focused on prices and, for the Chinese in particular, that they are instinctively commerce oriented. This opinion is quite common in the West, but it also comes out regularly when we conduct qualitative surveys like focus groups among Asians. The general truisms about price abound:

*". . . we Asians are always looking for the cheapest price."*

*"I go [to various shops] to check and compare prices."*

*"I [go there] just for browsing, their prices are usually higher."*

*". . . mainly, what [we Asians] look at is the price."*

*"[Asian] customers say they want to choose the patterns and designs, but when they're here, they just choose the price."*

If there is unanimous opinion, the cliché must be true. Or is it? How authentic are those comments; are they superficial or deeply rooted? Is there a self-fulfilling prophecy?

## Poor people need low prices

Here is an illustration from China. The city is Kunming in southwest China, but it could be almost any other place in that country. If you go to supermarkets or to supercenters in the city, especially if it's early in the morning, you can see a large proportion of elderly people in the stores. It is not that the elderly people have a particular experience or familiarity with hypermarkets, but they have something valuable—time. And as they are senior citizens their travel is generally subsidized by the city governments, so in many cases they don't pay when they take a bus.

What do you do when you have plenty of time and when you can travel freely in town? If you are an elderly Chinese, you go shopping. Or at least you go exploring. After breakfast (sometimes senior people have breakfast together in one of the public parks), each one goes to a destination. Some will go to a Walmart supercenter in the south of town to review the price of oil. Others will take the bus to explore the downtown Carrefour and will check out how much the eggs cost. Another will go to the supercenter called Trustmart to find other interesting prices. They will review the prices of the day, and, at a certain time, will come back to their starting point, the public park, and then exchange tips on which stores offer which deals on specific items.

What is the real value of these shoppers, for a retailer? Not too much because older people don't spend much. Their budgets are limited. The elder generations are very focused on prices; for them as for many other shoppers in the country, every penny counts.

There is a well-known cliché in the world of marketing: *Poor people need low prices, and rich people love low prices.*

This saying applies in Asia, too. The average Japanese customer may be much richer than the average Chinese, but prices in Japan are also four or five times higher. As the notion of being poor or being rich is extremely diverse in Asia, it is worth addressing the issue of disposable income. As we indicated in Chapter 1, we identified the average income levels of middle class households in the main Asian cities as well as many smaller towns, both in emerging countries and developed markets in the Far East. In a nutshell we could say the middle classes we surveyed are the Asian families who shop quite regularly at hypermarkets or supermarkets and at department stores from time to time, such as at least once a month. They are not the super rich but they are not poor.

## Price: the sole reason for selecting a store?

There is a very simple question that you can ask shoppers in various stores and in various countries, "Why do you shop at this store?" Respondents are generally interviewed after purchase so whoever answers is an actual shopper; they have physically bought something, they are not just walking by or browsing; and whatever they answer, their shopping visit is still fresh in their minds.

Their response will logically depend on where we conduct the interview. For customers at department stores or at category killers selling electric appliances, home improvement, or sporting goods, their answer is not purely related to prices and this is understandable. After all, if Asian customers go to a department store they expect to find the same products at the same prices as in other department stores, because in their minds the offer and the prices are controlled and standardized by the brand owners. The pricing is not a significant differentiator for most category killers either. At Toys'R'Us an Asian customer does not expect to find low prices for a Barbie doll. Shoppers go to the big-box specialists because they have a project or a specific product in mind, not primarily to find cheap products.

At the other extreme, if we interview shoppers in small outlets like convenience stores or small mom-and-pop shops, the customers will answer they came here because it is next door or because it is easy to reach the shop, not particularly because of the prices. So for these types of stores too, the price is not the main issue. In the case of wet markets or traditional markets, the customers also go there because of proximity to home and because of perceived freshness, not just because of prices.

However, with a hypermarket we would certainly expect the shoppers to mention low price as the major motivation. Hypermarkets and superstores are by definition the retail establishments that offer everything under one roof at low prices. Asians have a reputation for being very sensitive about price, so when we interview them in a hypermarket, we may expect most respondents to say they shop here because it is cheap. Furthermore, when we ask the question, "why do you shop here?" we accept all the answers the respondents can think of. Since we do not prompt and we accept multiple answers, we could theoretically anticipate that perhaps 95 percent or even 100 percent of Asian shoppers would mention *price*, or *cheap*, or *not costly*, as at least one among several reasons.

Let's review the outcome country by country. In Korea and Japan, just about 35 percent of the customers say the reason they shop a discount store or hypermarket is due to price. And price is not first; it's not even the second factor. The main reason is choice (or assortment) in Korea, and proximity to home in Japan and vice versa for reason number two. For Chinese markets, in the more developed countries like Singapore or Taiwan, the ratio is very similar: about 40 percent mention the price level a reason to visit. In both markets, choice is actually the main reason to come, and near home is second. A ratio of about 35 to 40 percent for price being one of the main reasons for shopping an outlet is not negligible of course, but it is not as dominant as we might expect.

In less developed countries such as China, the ratio is somewhat higher. About 50 percent of the hypermarket shoppers mention prices, but even then the major reason is not price, it is choice. Price is number two. It is basically the same ratio in most cities in Mainland China, whether it is Tianjin, Shanghai, Beijing, Kunming, or Chengdu, and whether customers reside in a relatively rich or a poor neighborhood. In Southeast Asia other than Singapore, the shoppers saying they come to hypermarkets for the prices amount to slightly above 50 percent, and here too the number one reason is something else than price. Most of the time, it is proximity to home. In markets like Vietnam, Cambodia, or Laos, price even rates a little below 50 percent for most product categories. However, we surveyed a limited number of outlets in those countries.

In effect, there is a divide in Asia about prices. When more than half of the shoppers say they come to a hypermarket because of prices we can safely conclude that price is at least "very" important. But in countries where just above one third are driven by prices, we need to consider what other reasons dominate. As a matter of fact, in Asian markets, the most important reasons relate to practicalities. Shoppers go to their supercenter or hypermarket because of proximity ("near my home" or "near my workplace") and also because of assortment or choice (the everything-under-one-roof concept).

So far we cannot really say that "Asians purely look for the lowest prices," because price is never the main reason mentioned and often, is not even among the top two. On the contrary we could actually hypothesize that perhaps Asian shoppers want to save time since they favor hypermarkets that don't require too much travel (proximity) and where a single shopping trip provides everything they need (assortment).

## Caveat about price satisfaction

Even if price is not the overwhelming reason for selecting a store, it is often number three in Asia. So retail chains are right to be concerned about the price image of their outlets and in most cases, store managers have some flexibility on pricing and can react locally. They check the prices competitors offer and they adjust. Chains also regularly commission customer interviews to measure the satisfaction, especially about prices.

This can be measured in a number of ways. We can ask shoppers about their price satisfaction, by ratings. For example, mark from 1 to 9, or with statements such as "very dissatisfied with prices" up to "very satisfied with prices." We can also ask comparative questions, whether shoppers feel this store is "much cheaper than elsewhere," "somewhat cheaper," and then identify what other stores the customers compare with—what is the "elsewhere" they have in mind.

A price image can also be specified by product categories, food (or even specific families in the food category like dry grocery, beverage), clothing (or even families in the garment category), etc.

Whenever we perform such a survey in Asia, we have to be cautious about the format and the competitive pressure. If we simply ask about price satisfaction, we generally have good news. In a convenience store, customers are happy with the price because an average ticket there is equivalent to one or two dollars. The prices are actually up to 11 percent higher than with hypermarkets for packaged goods, but even in a medium city in China or Southeast Asia, the shoppers feel they did not spend much anyway, so price was not a significant issue. For department stores, as we mentioned above, customers think the prices of branded items are standardized and around 60 percent of shoppers say they are satisfied with the prices because they don't see the same product being cheaper elsewhere. The same applies for category killers. Supermarkets are more expensive than hypermarkets, generally by 3 to 6 percent, but they also show about 60 percent satisfaction. It is logical that a customer says he is satisfied with prices because he shops there. If he said he is dissatisfied with prices but still shops there, he would feel odd as we indicated earlier with the principle of charity.

So, instead of satisfaction only, we can ask the comparative question, such as "Do you feel this store is much cheaper than elsewhere, somewhat cheaper than elsewhere?" We then explore from a different perspective and we no longer have a 60 percent general rating. For modern trade category killers for instance, only 10 percent or so of the customers will say the prices are cheaper than other places (either much cheaper or somewhat cheaper), while roughly 40 percent consider the prices are about the same and the rest say the category killer where they shop is more expensive than elsewhere. Category killers do business in Asia, but their customers don't go there for the prices and don't consider those stores to be inexpensive.

Hypermarkets on the other hand, aim for low prices. Roughly speaking, they show about 40 percent "cheaper than elsewhere" ratings, with another 50 percent saying the prices are similar to other places. Whenever a hypermarket has only 15 or 20 percent "cheaper than elsewhere" rating, this is a very bad sign. It does not matter if most of the remaining 80 or 85 percent say the prices are the same as elsewhere, this hypermarket is on the verge of failure. Such stores should never rate as low as 20 percent on the "cheaper than elsewhere" question. In the case of category killers, and department stores, this rating is not critical.

In Asian cities the competitive density is high, so most hypermarkets will have at least one competitor, with a catchment area that overlaps. It may happen however that a hypermarket enjoys a quasi monopoly in its trading zone, either because new laws prohibit expansion by competitors or because there is no available land to open a new outlet. In this circumstance a hypermarket can sell at relatively high prices with products costing more than they do at other stores with the same banner. Yet this hypermarket will show a strong score on the "cheaper than elsewhere" question because local competition is limited to small mom-and-pop shops and supermarkets with a higher pricing structure. This is rare but when it happens, the store is very profitable and the customer is not the winner in this configuration.

## Price sensitivity

If we look at price, not from an overall store image point of view, but from a customer behavior standpoint, we need to know which types of products Asian shoppers will buy according to the cost of the items—when they are really price-focused—and for which products price doesn't matter too much. This is what we will call price sensitivity.

Ideally this should be analyzed for each product category for food (fruit and vegetable, meat, fish, dry grocery, beverage) and non-food items (clothing, big appliances, small appliances, furniture). We can use several ways to measure price sensitivity. We can ask directly for what items customers care very much or not very much about prices. We can ask examples of products for which customers might decide to change store based on prices. We can ask in a given store which items are seen as particularly cheap or particularly expensive, and then look at the number of quotations. If product A is mentioned by many respondents, either as cheap or as expensive, it may imply that product A is price-sensitive. We also can use a combination.

In the Far East, responses show that people are almost always sensitive to the price of fresh products. Fresh includes fruit and vegetables, meat (mostly beef), fish, and bakery as well as prepared dishes when stores offer take-away foods. For some retailers, packaged goods like dairy or yogurt also belong to the fresh category.

In Japan and Korea, shoppers pay much attention to the price of fruit and vegetables, then meat (mostly beef). Other fresh items such as fish, sushi/sashimi, tofu or chicken are less price-sensitive because for those, the Korean and Japanese shoppers care essentially about quality and freshness, especially for fish, in Japan.

In Chinese markets on the other hand (Taiwan, China, and even Singapore), bread and cakes are among the most price-sensitive products together with fruit and vegetables. Chinese shoppers are also responsive to perceived quality but the price, for bakery in particular, is crucial, at the same level as for fruit and vegetables. Essentially, this is because something like bread is not part of the food culture and, if it's not a necessity, people will buy only when it's affordable. Also, unlike Japanese and Koreans, the Chinese shoppers are a little less sensitive about the price of meat and fish. As we'll see they care about the price of other items, in the packaged goods categories mostly.

If we look at shoppers in Southeast Asia, where the markets are mostly developing countries, excluding Singapore, customers are not extremely focused on the prices of produce, meat, fish or bakery. A relatively low price-sensitivity on fresh may seem quite strange for markets where shoppers are not rich, but this has to do with the natural conditions. In countries like the Philippines, Malaysia, Indonesia, Thailand, with extensive and diversified farmlands, people have access to local fresh foods at reasonable prices in wet markets. What the Southeast Asian customers look for is freshness. And when they buy at wet markets, they feel the produce is fresh.

For packaged goods, Koreans and Japanese focus on the price of cleaning products and grocery items, and the cost of beverages (non-alcohol). They think the quality is a given because they trust that a soda or a detergent in a store will be as good as the same brand item in another store, so for these packaged goods, the price is the dominant parameter.

It is slightly different in Chinese markets, where customers are sensitive to the price of packaged goods too, but particularly choosy about soap, detergents, and washing liquids. The perceived quality for those is not as straightforward as in Japan or Korea. Cleaning products in markets like China and Taiwan are not too price-sensitive because shoppers want to make sure they buy good products. In Southeast Asia, the situation is relatively simple in the sense that customers care about the prices in a similar way for all packaged goods.

When it comes to non-food in north Asia, the Koreans and Japanese don't pay too much attention to prices, much less than for fresh and dry goods. The only non-food items for which the cost will be important are big appliances such as white goods. Here again quality is not too much of an issue because they tend to feel the locally manufactured household appliances are of high quality.

For Chinese markets, big appliances appear as the main non-food item category that is price-sensitive. The others where price really matters in the non-food category are lamps and lighting sets. Are the Chinese customers sensitive to quality for the household appliances? The answer depends on how sophisticated the Chinese market is. In Singapore and Taiwan, the quality of brown goods and white goods sold in stores is not an issue and customers are not suspicious about quality, but in Mainland China, the customers do not always rely on the brands nor the producers for appliances. In traditional cities in south China (which does not mean small cities and does not mean that the residents are poor) like Guangzhou or Chongqing, customers are more suspicious and think deeply about the quality before purchasing appliances. In more modern cities like Shanghai, the shoppers focus less on the quality of household appliances. In Southeast Asia, big appliances are also the only non-food item for which customers are very much price oriented.

## A tale about psychological price and price elasticity

Unlike the paragraphs above, price elasticity is not just about "for what products does price matter to you?" It's also about "what will you do if we modify the price?" There are several methods to measure price elasticity. One of the most popular is, by convention, to start by reviewing a psychological price—what is the perceived price of a product. For this, we ask four questions:

*At what price is [product A] too expensive to consider purchase?*

*Beginning at what price is it expensive but you would still consider purchase? Beginning at what price is it cheap?*

*At what price is it so cheap you would doubt its quality?*

This gives benchmarks and when the answers to questions about "too expensive" and "too cheap" converge, the point of convergence is called optimal price. Then, if we ask some additional questions, we can perform a statistical treatment to forecast how much more sales, or less sales, we can achieve if we increase or decrease the price by so much.

Some examples of psychological price in Asia may look counter-intuitive. For instance, you might test two new cosmetics or perfumes. Both may have comparable high-quality packaging and similar container shape and capacity. Both have the same production cost, but with a different positioning. One, positioned as seductive for sexy girls, we'll call Seduce (not the real name). The other, more oriented toward young girls, we'll code-name Lolita (not the real name).

When you measure the answers to the four questions, you find that the optimal price for Seduce is higher than for Lolita. Yet both of the products may have great scores. In terms of logo (Lolita even rates a little better than Seduce), fragrance (Lolita also rates slightly higher than Seduce), and attractiveness of the packaging (again, Lolita may have a somewhat better score). To the question about how much each cosmetic and its packaging motivates the potential buyer, again both are rated almost equivalent with Lolita having a slightly better mark.

The irony is that when it comes to the elasticity questions, the product that has slightly better scores, Lolita, shows nevertheless a lower psychological price according to the Asian respondents. This looks odd. Except if you remember that Asian shoppers are first-degree.

Here the female respondents did not evaluate the optimal price based on the scent of the cream or the bottles or the outer packaging, because they had one guideline that was much more tangible. The Lolita positioning, for an Asian respondent, evokes either a young woman or a student. It makes reference to someone who is not a child but who does not have a career, at least not yet, and who does not earn much money; therefore the product should not be too costly. Seduce on the other hand, suggests a more sophisticated lady; therefore it is for wealthier people. Based on this perception, it makes sense that the psychological price would be a little higher.

Price elasticity is a slightly different subject. Although this book does not aim to explain in detail how price elasticity is calculated, we can briefly mention that we measure how much customers like the products that are probed. We also measure whether they feel the products are attractive, satisfying, necessary, appropriate, and so forth. The results show the Asian customers' way of thinking about the products and ultimately about the prices.

Price elasticity can be measured for various items, from baby pacifiers to PDAs, and results are generally quite logical. For example, if you reduce the retail price by 3 percent you can achieve 6 percent more volume sold, which sounds good. If you increase the price by 2 percent you lose 2 percent volume in return, which sounds neutral. Retailers or brand owners then use these results to fine-tune their pricing policies whether they want to gain market share or increase profits.

However, if you want to increase profits your strategy will not be to reduce price by 3 percent and gain 6 percent more volume. This is because if you originally sold at 100 a product that cost you 50, you earned 5,000 for every 100 units sold. If you decide to retail at 97, your margin is now 47 per unit. Even though you will sell 106 units instead of 100, you will earn only 106 x 47, which is less than the 5,000 you made before. The "reduce price by 3 percent and gain 6 percent more volume" option sounded good, but it was not very profitable. On the other hand if the retailer or the producer wants to improve market share, reducing price by 3 percent can be a good decision.

A strange elasticity result may occur when we probe something like the Rubik's cube in Asia. The product we test can be a standard Rubik's 3x3, shrink wrapped, or an equivalent. We are interviewing female shoppers, with higher than average household income and with at least one child below 16 years of age.

What we can find with the price elasticity of such a product is that if you raise the price by 3 or 4 or 5 percent, you virtually don't lose volumes. You can achieve 99 units sold instead of 100. Conversely if you reduce the price by 4 percent you can sell 112 units for every 100 you used to. This means 12 percent more volume if you reduce the price by only 4 percent. In this circumstance, it's worth thinking about it if you are the brand owner or the retailer.

The point for this kind of item is that it does not rate particularly high on the questions probing whether it is attractive or satisfying, but it has a high rating for "necessity." The respondents, Asian mothers, feel that a product like this can be one of the elements that will develop intelligence for their children; therefore it's a necessary item. This is linked with the notion of hard work and education. Such a toy has an educational value and is seen as a tool to make the kids smarter. It also illustrates that Asian parents have ambition for their children.

All those examples tend to demonstrate that Asian customers do not always make purchase decisions based solely on retail price, and stores should not purely focus on being the cheapest, not to mention that a bleeding strategy in rarely fruitful.

## Price and value for money

So far we briefly touched upon the subject of quality and price but did not specify if there is such a thing as a price-quality ratio. The concept of PQR is often used when it's not easy to measure quality. For a microchip, quality is easy to gauge. Either the circuitry works or it doesn't and generates a certain amount of heat, which can be measured. However, in the world of food, wine, or spirits, for example, it's not so straightforward. A whisky connoisseur may disregard blended whiskies and may absolutely love his favorite single malt Scotch because his taste buds tell him this complex spirit is mellow and because his nose will sense various fragrances. This connoisseur weighs the perceived quality and the price, and will feel that his preferred bottle of single malt is absolutely worth the price he paid. With his taste buds, he made a judgment, which, for him, is a price-quality ratio. In Asia we'd say there is no such thing. Taste buds don't count.

An Asian customer of wine, whisky or cognac is likely to buy one bottle or another based on social considerations, for instance because he wants to honor a client, or because it gives face. For him the personal judgment about PQR does not apply; he will buy what is socially encouraged. So, if he is a businessman at a nightclub for instance, if it is appropriate to order a bottle of cognac XO, that's what he'll ask for. And if the nightclub offers a one-liter bottle for the price of 70 cl, the notion that applies is not price quality ratio. It's value for money.

You may feel that it's not entirely fair to believe that many Asians are not very discriminating, by comparing a whisky connoisseur and a simple businessman. One is qualified as a wine and spirits professional, while the other cannot be considered as a wine specialist. In fact the same type of comment can be made about fresh fruit, tea, ground coffee or virtually any food item. In the last 50 years or so, Asian countries have been focused on developing the economy and, with urbanization, people have more and more lost touch with nature and farm products. Let's take China for instance: thirty years ago, Mainland China was essentially a rural country. Now, in 2011–2012, half of the people in the country are city dwellers. And in thirty years' time, another 300 million Chinese will reside in cities. During a human lifespan, China will evolve from a rural economy to a country where 65 percent of the population lives in urban zones.

Half a century ago, the ethnologist Claude Levi-Strauss acknowledged the fact that age-old societies, from the Philippines to the Ruykyu Islands, had "an intimate familiarity with local plants and a precise knowledge of plant classification," with a botanical vocabulary of 2,000 words (The Savage Mind, University of Chicago Press, 1968). Today most people in Asia can perhaps talk more easily about the stock exchange than about botanicals. Instead of whisky, we can make a parallel with betel nuts, a local "sin product" in Asia. The market for betel nuts is quite significant. It represents several billion dollars at retail and a yearly production of more than one million metric tons. The betel nut, also known as areca nut or pinang, is a traditional stimulant that can hamper health and is grown in several countries in the Far East. Millions of end-consumers in Greater China and Southeast Asia chew various types of betel nuts regularly, but unlike their ancestors, they are not able to cite the different varieties of areca nuts nor the substitutes. The Asian customers of today, whether they buy typical local products at traditional retail or fresh produce or other foods at modern trade, do not always have the vocabulary or the background to judge quality and to be discriminating about what they eat, drink or taste.

We think value in Asia essentially needs to be quantifiable. The customer doesn't know whether the bottle of XO cognac is higher quality than a 20-year single malt whisky, and the same would apply to traditional local products, as the betel nut example. But what he knows is that today, the bottle of XO is recommended by sales staff and is offered with a promotion. This is visible and quantifiable.

## How Asians define quality

We can review some examples of links between price, quality, and value. In all Asian markets, as we have seen, customers pay attention to the price of fresh food, so it is worth addressing how Asian shoppers also define quality for fresh. One of the findings is that Asians differentiate between the notion of quality and the notion of freshness. Therefore, it would be a mistake for a retailer to think quality equals freshness. An apple or a mango can be fresh but not tasty or not sweet enough and vice versa. Furthermore, Asian customers will sometimes say the traditional markets offer freshness but not necessarily quality, and that conversely, a given supermarket rates better on quality of fresh produce than it rates on freshness of the produce.

What is quality versus freshness in their view? Quality partly refers to taste, of course, like everywhere else: "The meat has to be savory, not bland; the vegetable has to taste good after it's cooked; the fruit must be sweet." But taste in Asia is not the only criterion, and not even the main element. It is just one among several criteria on quality, which often correspond to things that are visible, or tangible. For example, some Asian customers will need to see a guarantee of some sort: "In this store, there is a safety guarantee" or "There is no quality guarantee at the wet markets." Asian customers will also look at the color: "The meat has to have luster, the fruit must be bright and shiny, the vegetables need to be green not yellow." In effect, when asked directly how they judge quality for fresh food, Asian customers answer, "Mainly by observation of the products, the luster, brightness in color." Quality is judged by observation.

The Asian customers we interviewed, when talking about the notion of freshness, as opposed to quality, often refer to criteria that are tangible too. It can be very simple: "Fresh is when the expiry date is not passed." Fresh, in the case of meat, will mean the animal "was slaughtered today," or "produced and sold on the same day." For vegetables in Asia, fresh is also sometimes misunderstood: "The produce was not chilled, no refrigeration." For freshness, too, Asian customers judge by what they see, or they rely on codes, which are more or less prejudgments: "If (pork) is hanging, it must be fresh;" "vegetables on a counter are more fresh," as opposed to vegetables that are not displayed loose on a counter. The way to judge freshness also denotes a level of suspicion: "Pre-packed, sometimes, they are rotten but you cannot see."

These pre-perceptions that we consider "first degree" can be misleading and even disputed. For example butchers and nutritionists will say that one should not eat meat that is too fresh. The idea that "the animal should be slaughtered today" is actually not a good one because the meat would still contain too much water and the nerves would be too hard.

It is preferable for the meat to be several days old before it is consumed, both to avoid problems of urea and for time to make it more tender and savory. A steak or a pork chop that is two-days old, for instance, will be more watery than the same meat after one or two weeks maturation. Butchers and retailers often do not dispute the shoppers' first-degree pre-judgments because, among other reasons, contradicting customers is not good marketing.

There is one more parameter about freshness that is, it would seem, not exactly first-degree and is not based on what you see for yourself. It is the nutrition factor. Many Asian customers will tell our interviewers that products that are fresh are "more rich in nutrition." Up to a quarter of the shoppers may have this type of comment in the case of vegetables. Surely this means Asians are not so much first-degree after all, since they think about what will go into their bodies and they think about nutrition and health. This is partly true, but when we probe more deeply, we often find that the motivation is not purely health; it is cost.

*"If I buy a vegetable which is not fresh I have to cutoff those parts not fresh and there will be not much left, so it's less nutritious."*

In other words, if lack of freshness means you need to throw away 10 or 20 percent of the vegetable that you bought; it cost you 10 or 20 percent more. In this regard freshness is in fact a quantifiable notion. It is cost oriented.

## How local minorities perceive prices

In any given country in Asia, there are local minorities. Nearly one million people of Korean origin live in Japan for instance. Some ethnic groups have lived for centuries in a territory, such as in parts of China or Taiwan, where some of the people are often called aboriginals and constitute 2 or 3 percent of the population. In Asia there are religious minorities as well, especially Muslims in parts of the Philippines, Thailand, and China (3 to

5 percent of the population in each case). The Chinese are themselves a significant minority in countries like Malaysia (25 percent of the people) or Indonesia (about 4 or 5 percent). All minorities shop and consume in ways that are slightly different than the main residents. Not to mention that in some markets such as Hong Kong, Singapore, Thailand, foreigners who either reside or visit as tourists represent in effect a large minority too, as far as shopping is concerned.

Based on the surveys we have conducted, aboriginals are generally less well off than the others in a given country, with a household income that is 10 to 30 percent lower than the national average. They tend to spend a little more time working during weekdays and weekends and they watch TV a bit less and spend more time shopping than the average Chinese nationals. Time spent doesn't imply higher expenditure. In fact aboriginals consume less, especially on non-food (about 25 percent lower consumption). They also have a reputation for being stingy, but when we probe them, they show roughly the same attitude toward price and value for money as their neighbors who are Chinese. The only cases when their reputation of being extremely price-sensitive is verified is when it comes to expensive items. Aboriginals then feel that a high price and high quality product is not what they need. But this does not mean they have a different perception of value. It mostly reflects the attitude of customer groups who live with a relatively low income.

For Muslims in the parts of Asia where they live as a minority, there is a specific profile, too. They have larger families with approximately one more child than other households in the same country, and household incomes are about 10 percent lower. Their attitude to shopping is generally enthusiastic, in the sense that Muslims are more eager to try new shopping destinations than the average residents, especially in low-income areas. Again, this does not necessarily connote a specific cultural trait but is often due to the standard of living. When your income is low, you feel the existing stores are expensive and you expect that a new retail establishment will trigger competitive pricing. Muslims in the catchment areas that we probed are more price-sensitive than average for basic needs like fresh produce, packaged goods, and clothing, but for other items such as appliances or homewares their attitude to price is the same as the other Asian inhabitants in a given territory.

As for the foreigners, if we focus on Westerners, they appear to be less sensitive to price than Asians or at least more easily satisfied with pricing. If a survey shows for instance that 10 percent of the Asian customers are very satisfied with the prices, on a same store basis, the same survey shows that 20 percent of the foreign shoppers are very satisfied.

Next we touch upon the promotional offers, which are an important part of the shopping equation in Asia.

# 6

# The Ambiguities of Promotions

MODERN trade in Asia today provides the same kinds of promotions as modern trade in the West. A promotion can be as simple as a price reduction. It can also be complex, such as offering cash rewards or free talk time for your pre-paid cellphone, based on which participating products and brands you bought. There are lots of mechanics such as free additional quantity—buy two get one free, or get a larger pack sold at the original price. There are lucky draws, with which you buy something and have the chance to participate in a lottery of some sort. There are privileged events as well, such as midnight sales at a department store where only some specific customers can join and attend a preview or a fashion show and have the opportunity to be the first in town to acquire the products. There are cash coupons and gifts with purchase, co-promotions with credit card companies, and loyalty programs with which you accumulate points and redeem something later.

The types of promotions are similar as in the rest of the world but the customer attitude is not always the same as in Western markets. There are ambiguities.

## If it's on promotion, it must be bad

The first ambiguity with promotions in Asia is that the promotional concept itself is on a collision course with old pre-judgments. In the past, even just one generation ago, if an Asian producer or a store did a promotion, many customers thought there was probably something wrong with the merchandise. It was quite a spontaneous and universal suspicion.

*". . . if they promote it, it's because the product doesn't sell by itself, therefore it has a flaw."*

Today, we still find this negative connotation but it's mostly among the less developed markets, where even a thirty-five or forty-year-old house-wife will sometimes feel that a promotion is probably "hiding" something. In part, this is an expression of seeing-is-believing, but it is also an effect of real experience from the past, when local retailers tried to sell the success-ful products at high prices and had to discount steeply the merchandise that was not popular.

With the spread of modern trade and international packaged goods (and the promotional approach that followed), this pre-perception is no longer dominant. In most cases in Asia today, shoppers who are younger than age 60 appreciate special offers and are not as suspicious as their elders. A promotion is no longer associated with a risk.

However, we have to differentiate between *fast moving consumer goods* (FMCG), groceries, or personal care, and the slow moving items, such as electrical appliances or garments. When Asian shoppers purchase FMCG they buy their usual products, which are often international brands. In any case, those are items they feel confident with, in terms of quality and brand recognition. What they will do is check the best-before date when relevant and select carefully the items with an expiry date that's far away, but they will not have doubts about their international brand of milk or shampoo. In this case a promotion is welcome. If an Asian female shopper likes to buy a specific shampoo and today her brand is on promotion, she will purchase it and possibly stock up on some additional units, but she will not have second thoughts about the special offer.

When it comes to durable products however, or products where brand awareness and image are not prominent, typical shoppers in many Asian countries may still be suspicious when they see a promotion. Why? Let's take the example of furniture. In Asia, there are no major furniture brands, and the retail chains are not perceived as brands, except for Ikea. If customers want to buy a set of table and chairs or a bed, there is no strong brand name to reassure them. The same is true for lamps and for various decoration elements and accessories. So how do Asian shoppers react to a promotion in the case of durable goods with low brand recognition or no brand name? Actually it depends on the use of the goods. In the case of a table, a bed, or a mattress, Asian customers are not sensitive to the brand name because they have a low brand awareness, and are not too focused on quality (for them a table is a table, a mattress is a mattress, but it is fair to say they pay attention to the design and the look).

For those products with no significant differentiation; Asian shoppers are very interested in the promotions and the concern about quality is secondary. Conversely, for items like bathroom accessories or lighting sets, customers care about the reputation of the maker and prefer to buy a brand that is well known, or at least one that signifies quality and safety. In this case the shoppers will be a little less promotion-oriented, and a little more focused on the perceived quality and positioning of the slow-moving products they buy, and they may be distrustful of a promotion. They may think the promoted item is coming from old stocks for instance. The level of suspicion toward promotional offers is less significant in Korea and Japan, but more present in Southeast Asia. In countries like Thailand, Malaysia, the Philippines, or Indonesia it makes sense for category killers for instance, if they do not sell FMCG, to be careful with promotions and for some product categories, to consider the approach called *every day low price* or EDLP.

## High-low and EDLP

There are two main philosophies in the retail world about pricing and promotions. One is called *high-low*, which means selling products generally at a regular price point (considered high price) and then offering a discount periodically (which is then the low price). With this approach, Asian shoppers can see the difference. It is clearly noticeable because the original price is written on a yellow fluorescent board and is slashed with the discounted price written next to it. Even with a small rebate, shoppers can see unmistakably that there is a price cut. In some Asian countries, supermarkets and hypermarkets proudly showcase a price cut equivalent to a few U.S. cents. Stores are usually following the high-low principle and all the customers can see the discounted offers of the day or the week on TV, in the press, or through the brochures they receive at home. The advantage of high-low is its attractiveness. There is always some kind of surprise, always some bargains at the high-low store; it's fun and it generates traffic. The drawback is logistics. It is technically a complication for the chain to organize all this. Retailers must calculate how many items can theoretically be sold with a certain promotion, how much quantity they need to order, organize the promotional communication, decide how to react if they did not order enough, or conversely if they ordered too much.

Unlike high-low, the EDLP, sounds simpler and appears as sort of a long term unwritten contract with the customers. The every-day-low-price store says to shoppers that the prices will be always as low as possible and although some promoted items can be cheaper elsewhere, what counts is the total basket of goods bought. Indirectly it says the high-low approach is not in the best interest of customers since they have to pay the "high" price for too many items.

EDLP is also quite simple to manage in terms of logistics and seems to generate trust. Up to a point Asian shoppers can see that the EDLP store, in theory, does not spend much on communication about promotional offers (no need to produce and distribute thousands of brochures, no expensive print ads in newspapers, no TV commercials). Shoppers can therefore understand the idea that the EDLP stores offer low prices thanks to all the savings since there is less marketing expenditure.

The drawback of every-day-low-price, generally speaking, is that it lacks excitement. Therefore, the issue is whether or not shoppers in Asia want excitement, whether they feel what they need from a store is just EDLP, or whether they want to be surprised by slashed prices, by products displayed on promotional podiums, and by brochures in their mail.

In Asia today, EDLP is more of a slogan than a marketing philosophy. Many stores use signboards with the every-day-low-prices message while in fact, the approach is simply high-low. There is however a real difference in China, for example, where both Walmart and Carrefour operate. Carrefour has always been perceived as a high-low concept. Walmart is traditionally EDLP. Many professionals say that Carrefour does better than Walmart in China because its top 10 hypermarkets show higher sales turnovers than Walmart's top ten stores. In reality, this is mostly due to the size of the outlets (Carrefour in China has bigger stores on average). It is also due to the high-low approach, since a typical Carrefour hypermarket aims for a large catchment area and through promotions, wants to attract shoppers from as far away as possible. A Walmart store on the other hand will tend to operate on a smaller geographic zone and appears to aim for loyal customers using EDLP and other strategies. At the end of the day, both high-low and EDLP can work and can be profitable for a chain. We will come back to this in the chapter on Asian customer loyalty.

## Promotion with deferred benefit

There is a second ambiguity about promotions, which is the meaning of the word itself, since there are various mechanics. As we said, almost all retailers in Asia like to use the phrase EDLP because it sounds nice, but in effect they provide high-low, up to a point. The types of promotions that follow the high-low method are quite diversified, but we can divide this into two groups, whether the benefit is obtained immediately, such as a gift incentive, or whether it comes later—a point collection system for instance.

We interviewed Asian shoppers about promotions in various types of stores (supermarkets and hypermarkets, department stores, sporting goods specialists, category killers of appliance or furniture, home improvement, toys retailers, etc). The results are quite homogeneous among countries, but vary depending on what kind of store we examine.

First, Asian customers appreciate both the immediate effect and deferred effect promotions, but in diverse degrees. If we look at promotions with deferred effect, three mechanics generally prevail: **cash coupons, point collection systems,** and **lucky draws.**

The **cash coupon** approach is loved. At supermarkets in particular, about 65 to 70 percent of shoppers will say they like cash coupons. It is nearly the same with department stores. About 55 to 60 percent of their customers like the cash coupons, slightly more when the department store is located in a zone where lower middle classes reside. With category killers like furniture or electrical appliance specialists, or at sporting goods retailers, the cash coupon appreciation is lower, just around 50 percent, and it can be as low as 25 percent in any market, for the upper-income shoppers who buy at upscale category killers, even in China. Upscale shoppers who are buying non-food (home improvement materials or high-quality toys for their children, for instance) are not looking for a cash coupon but they don't reject those either. For general merchandise, Asian customers of all income groups appreciate the cash coupon. It is concrete, it is visible, and it means money.

The deferred promotion mechanics that are much less liked are the **point collection** systems such as membership (liked by only 30 percent at non-food and 50 to 55 percent at food retail). Many chains develop membership programs for two reasons. One is to make shoppers loyal by giving points and benefits. The other goal is to track the purchase records of each customer and over time try to accurately understand their needs. This second goal often called CRM for customer relationship management is a means to better know the customers and better serve them. The approach was very well explained by Humby and Hunt writing about Tesco (*Scoring Points: How Tesco Continues to Win Customer Loyalty,* Kogan Page, 2008).

Diapers can illustrate how CRM works. If a customer buys diapers for a baby of a certain age, the store can infer this customer's household has a child of that age; therefore it should be possible to sell her baby food for the corresponding age as well. The retailer can design a tailor-made offer for this household to encourage the purchase of baby food at their stores. Since the customer groups are clearly identified as qualified targets, it makes sense to send this specific offer to them. The store sees this as a win-win operation since the household needs to purchase the baby food anyway, so if there is a special offer in the process, the family would be happy and the store would increase sales. However, some Asian mothers do not fully appreciate this as they feel it is intrusive.

The other effect of the membership card is the accumulation of points, which over time also constitutes a benefit. In less-developed countries like Indonesia the point collection is not sophisticated and does not always involve a member card *per se* but will consist of stamp collections based on amounts of purchase, and customers receive some deferred benefit. Although 50 to 55 percent of Asian customers like the point collection at food retail, versus 65 to 70 percent who like cash coupons, there are also some customers who dislike them. Whereas nearly everybody likes cash coupons, about 15 percent of Asian shoppers do not like the point collections. Some say a membership card system is too complicated and requires time to accumulate points; others consider CRM too pushy.

The remaining 30 percent or so are customers who are ambivalent and do not pay much attention to the point collection system. They don't formally dislike the method but feel it is tedious and that following up is not really worth it after all. Therefore, some stores try to make the process as simple as possible for shoppers. For instance, if a customer forgot her member card, she can simply tell the cashier her phone number when paying, and the computer system will identify the customer data and credit the points. This approach works well from a technical standpoint, but it has some limits culturally, in particular in Muslim countries with female shoppers because for this customer group "a good girl doesn't give her phone number," even for the good cause. Even for a promotion.

The **lucky draw** is another promotional method with deferred effect, as it offers a chance to participate in a lottery upon buying specific products. Response to the lucky draw is lukewarm. Only a little more than 35 percent of shoppers appreciate it in the case of food retail and it is even a bit less than 35 percent if the retailer is a category killer. Westerners sometimes believe that since Asians are superstitious and they like fun activities, they will love a lucky draw. Actually more often than not, Asian customers will say, "I don't like lucky draws, I have bad luck" or "I don't want to wait for the lucky draw" because most of the time they don't feel today is a lucky day and they don't perceive a store lottery as entertainment. As a matter of fact our surveys show that about 20 percent clearly dislike this promotional technique.

How should we interpret the percentages? If 20 percent answer that they don't like lucky draws for instance, does it still mean the other 80 percent are at some level eager or at least willing to participate? And if 35 percent say they do like the mechanics, can we conclude that it's not too bad? We interpret the customer feedback with Confucius in mind, especially the sense of harmony. If 20 percent say, "No I don't like," this is already quite clearly negative, because Asians don't say "no" superficially. And if 35 percent say, "I like this type of promotion," we need to probe more deeply.

For lucky draws, our surveys show that only 10 to 12 percent like them "very much," while 20 to 25 percent "somewhat like it" (which is an indirect way to say they are quite neutral). We also have approximately 45 percent who are officially neutral, as they answer "neither like nor dislike." We need to be cautious when Asian shoppers say "neither/nor" on a subject because, unless they really don't know the issue, it's generally a polite way to show a distance with the topic. In our judgment, if 20 percent Asian customers say clearly "no," and only 10 to 12 percent say strongly "yes," with a huge majority being neutral or semi-neutral, it means at best that 12 percent like the offer, and potentially 88 percent will stay on the sidelines.

In the case of promotions with deferred effect, the fact that you will collect points or have a chance to win at the lottery involves too much uncertainty and Asian customers much prefer tangibility and visibility, not "uncertain" benefits. Cash coupons are quite appreciated because of their palpable nature.

## Country variations

There are some differences by countries. Based on our surveys, it seems to us that the Chinese, in Mainland China but also in Hong Kong and Taiwan, especially when they reach a higher than average level of income, are more impatient and even less likely to appreciate deferred promotions. Conversely, in parts of China where the residents have lower incomes, the appreciation of something like a lucky draw is a little higher than average. In some parts of Indonesia too, we found that customers tend to accept more easily the deferred effect promotions, like the point collection systems. Even if it takes several months to accumulate enough points for rewards, as long as the benefit is equivalent to some cash, the somewhat cumbersome promotion method is still acceptable to the lower income shoppers. They are grateful and appreciate any kind of benefit. Generally, it appears that if an Asian market is emerging or still developing, such as most of China, the Philippines, Indonesia, and Vietnam for instance, shoppers are more thankful for the deferred promotions than customers in developed countries are. This is essentially due to low income and low exposure to sophisticated promotion mechanics.

In Thailand, more than elsewhere in Asia, people appear to be somewhat sensitive to the fun element of accumulating points or participating in a lottery. At similar income levels, and for a similar store type, slightly more Thai shoppers "like very much" the lucky draws than those who dislike them. This is as much a specific cultural trait of Thai people as it is due to the income levels that are still low.

## Promotions with immediate effect

Overall the deferred promotions, other than the cash coupons, are not a winning concept because even in emerging markets gifts and lucky draws show lower ratings than other mechanics and as customers will become more and more affluent, they will be less receptive, we think, to promotions with fun value. Actually, it is quite the same in Asia as in Europe and America. In the twenty-first century, people grow more impatient and want to see immediate results.

Across Asian countries shoppers say they do like offers of immediate rewards. A gift incentive is an immediate reward (buy a 70 cl. scotch whisky bottle, get a travel bag; buy a shower gel and get a small towel), and so is a free additional quantity (pay for the price of the 70 cl. but get a 1 liter bottle; get a larger pack of shower gel for the price of the regular size). In both cases Asian shoppers say very clearly, "I like this promotion"—up to 80 percent for the free additional quantity in the case of supermarkets and about 65 percent for the free gift or 65 percent for the additional quantity at non-food stores. However, if the customers have a higher income and purchase a valuable product, like a plasma TV or if they want to redecorate part of their home, the pertinence of the free gift or the free quantity could be quite secondary. A Chinese customer renovating his bathroom will be more interested in a lower down payment, for instance, than in three buckets of paint sold for the price of two, especially if he needs only two buckets. He is not going to spend time to try to resell the extra paint; he has other things to do. But as a general rule, the levels of appreciation are high with the free quantity and the gift incentive mechanics.

Yet, the really preferred promotion tactic is the discount, a plain and simple price reduction. This is the favored type of promotions across all types of stores; up to 90 percent of supermarket customers say they like discounts and above 80 percent among shoppers at department stores. At category killers the ratio is also extremely high, between 80 and 85 percent of the customers like to have a rebate, while the rest are neutral; virtually nobody will say, "don't like."

We asked Asian shoppers about their preference between a store that offers a steep discount for a limited number of items, versus many discounted products but each with a small rebate. If, for Asians, seeing is believing, what do they like to see in a store in terms of discounts?

We asked this question the same way in several countries. Granted, each respondent may have in mind a personal definition of what is "many" and how he or she considers a discount to be "steep" (usually the cutoff point is around 10 percent but it varies by product categories). Yet, the respondents in Asia all have a converging opinion. Their answer is always, "We prefer few promoted products with a high discount." This is the case for Asian females as well as males (slightly more so for females); it is the case whatever the age group or the income. A respondent with above average income prefers big discounts on a few selected items as much as the below average income respondent.

Such policy can be good for retailers because it widens the catchment area, as mentioned earlier. In Asia, shoppers who live about 20 minutes away will be about three times more likely to shop at the store having a steep discount approach for a selection of products, than a similar store focused on EDLP.

So, Asian customers are not necessarily impressed when they see a large number of items under promotion. If we refer to the rebates with the value of a few cents mentioned earlier, those "many items with a small discount" will not have a tremendous impact. But customers in the Far East will be impressed if they see at least a few products with a steep discount.

We do have to point out that in stores such as supermarkets, about one third of the shoppers do not actually notice the promotion materials. Fewer than half of the visitors look at the brochures made available in store (which is not necessarily the same as direct mail received at home) and when there are LCD screens in the store, fewer than half of the visitors look at those. Less than 40 percent look regularly at the posters or promotional signage in store as well. When a chain has a new campaign (ensuring low price or a promise to refund the difference if you find a cheaper product elsewhere, for instance) and wants to communicate more strongly, the result can be disappointing; about one-third of the customers will not even notice that there is a new policy or a new promotion.

## Are Asians different when it comes to promotions?

Do Asians have a different attitude than other customers in the world, about discounts and promotions?

In many Far East stores where we do customer interviews, some of the respondents are foreigners. At some department stores or upscale category killers for instance, the ratio of foreign visitors can reach 20 percent. If those visitors actually buy something, they are not browsers. By defini-tion, they are customers, and if we want our surveys to be representative of the actual customer flow, we need to interview them too. We cannot say those foreigners are representative of the West; generally they are either tourists or expatriates who live in Asia. However, when the outlet is relatively upscale, both the local and the foreign customer groups are middle or upper class. We can know this from their answers to questions about demographics like personal income, household income, education level, and occupation of the shopper or the head of household. If we have similar socio-economic backgrounds we can compare answers from local and foreign customers whenever we conduct a survey on a same store and same timing basis.

In terms of preference about promotions with deferred effect, both Asians and foreigners like coupons in the same proportion (about 55 percent at upscale non-food stores). Foreigners dislike the lucky draws and point collection systems even more than Asians, the difference being about 10 percentage points less. For promotions with immediate effect there is also a little difference. While at least 65 percent of Asians really appreci-ate receiving a gift incentive, the foreign shoppers are not so enthusiastic (about 10 percentage points less). Discount and free additional quantity are liked at the same level. It appears that foreigners distinguish perhaps more about which offers they really like or not, whereas Asians are rela-tively open to various types of promotions.

Other than the mechanics they prefer, there is a difference between Asian and foreign shoppers with regards to their actual satisfaction about the special offers they experience. As much as 50 percent of foreign shoppers may say they are satisfied or at least somewhat satisfied with promotions at a given non-food store for instance, but Asian customers would show only half of this ratio. This is a large difference.

So, if only 25 percent of Asian customers are satisfied with promotions, it means a very large proportion is at least discontented in some way about the special offer. When Asian shoppers explain they are dissatisfied with promotions, they often refer to the lack of exposure and the low motivation to visit a store. Lack of exposure does not occur too much for hypermarkets and supermarkets in Asia because these chains print brochures and various advertisements in profusion but some non-food retailers advertise less.

If customers don't have much opportunity to see a chain's print ads, TV commercials or to receive the brochures at home, they will say, "I don't get any news from them." It is not a question of awareness but exposure. Moreover, the execution of an ad has to be concrete and to show tangible benefits. The department store communication saying "up to 50 percent discounts on watches and writing instruments" is actually too vague for Asians because shoppers have no guarantee about which brands will be deeply discounted, and because nothing is shown precisely. If another promotional sign advertises a deep discount for men's casual wear, or ladies' shoes, or accessories, and Asian customers don't see which brands are involved, it is not concrete. The customers will not know if the promotion is really attractive and motivating.

The trigger has to be visible, tangible, and needs a call to action. In the studies we conducted it appears that the shoppers who feel the promotions don't happen frequently enough are actually, in large part, the ones who did not pay attention to the TV commercials or the newspaper print ads. For those shoppers, the brochure or the direct mails that they find in the mailbox and that show in detail a wide selection of promoted goods have more impact. The real issue in this case is the cost effectiveness between printing and delivering all those catalogues and leaflets, versus the return on investment. A chain in Asia that cuts the budget of direct mail probably makes a mistake.

Another difference between Asian and foreign customers when it comes to shopping has to do with the axiom "too much promotion kills the promotion." We probed in stores in various countries whether customers feel "there are too many promotions" in the store and offered five possible answers: totally agree, somewhat agree, neither-nor, somewhat disagree, totally disagree. Only 3 or 4 percent of the Asian customers will say they agree while more than 50 percent disagree with the statement. Clearly, they don't think there is too much promotion. In the same stores, 10 to 12 percent of the foreigners will think the store does too many promotions; less than 40 percent will disagree. This is a big variance. Asians still appear to be eager to experience special offers.

Asian Muslims have a similar attitude toward promotions as the other customers in Asia. They appreciate promotions on food but they also consider that it only saves a little bit of money; it is nice but not critical. And for non-food, especially in the case of high-ticket items like big appliances, for example, Muslims not only appreciate the promotions, but also consider a discount to be a major criterion for purchase (around 50 percent for other Asians, but about 55 percent for Asian Muslims).

## Loyalty to brands or loyalty to promotions

Now that we have established that shoppers in Asia favor promotions with immediate effect and that in the end, they simply prefer to enjoy a few steep discounts, there is a further ambiguity. Are Asian customers going to switch from brand to brand as long as they find a deep discount, or is there a limit to the enjoyment of discounts? And if a chain offers lots of attractive promotions, will shoppers tend to go to those stores or will they continue to shop at their usual place, even if their usual store follows the EDLP concept? The question here covers a dual issue. Will discounts have an effect on the customer loyalty toward the manufacturer's brands and also, will promotions impact loyalty to a store?

Customers in Asia have a reputation for not being loyal, be it to a brand or a retailer. In fact, the surveys we have conducted show that Asians are sensitive to promotions but they are probably more loyal to brands than their reputation says. When a manufacturer does a promotion, the customers are happy to purchase the promoted goods, but this mainly happens *if* they are used to buying those brands in the first place. In a majority of cases, the Asian shoppers may see a promotion but, if it is not their brand, will not buy the promoted item and will purchase their usual brand instead.

From our surveys at supermarkets with a number of product categories, it appears that about 60 percent of Asian shoppers will continue to buy their usual brand even when it's not on promotion, whereas 30 percent may switch and purchase a competitive product that is promoted. The rest are unsure or not answering. Among the 30 percent who may switch, only 3 percent answer they definitely will do so, while the other 27 percent say they'll probably buy the competitive product that is discounted. Such an answer is in no way a commitment and we can interpret this as a rather neutral answer.

In a department store of a mid-scale neighborhood, we have essentially the same proportions of 60 percent brand-loyals and 30 percent switchers, but customers of a more upscale department store would be a little more likely to switch in favor of the promoted brand—37 percent with 4 percent of definitely yes. A level of about 30 percent who may shift sounds high, but the customers who are really committed to switching based on a discount (3 or 4 percent) are not that numerous.

For shoppers of a category killer, many producer brands are often perceived as equivalent in terms of function and image. At electric appliance category killers for instance, we have 40 percent or slightly more who might switch (with about 10 percent definitely yes), depending on how clever and convincing the promotion is. It's approximately the same for home improvement and sporting equipment stores. When the brands are not differentiated or are even perceived as commodities, we reach 40 to 45 percent who might switch based on discount. Conversely when the category killer sells brands with high recognition and image, like international brands of toys or sports shoes, there are fewer switchers—only around 25 percent (with 6 or 7 percent definitely yes) versus 30 to 35 percent who would not switch brands even when there is a promotion.

The question of loyalty toward a store is also complex. Will shoppers cherry-pick from store to store in order to find the best promotion?

First, whatever the promotion policy, a customer will continuously shop the same store if the location is good, based on accessibility or proximity to home and other variables we addressed in Chapter 4. However, let's bear in mind that continuous shopping does not necessarily mean the customer is loyal (more on this in Chapter 9). Second, all else being equal, we have to consider the profile of the shopper. A store offering reasonable prices without many promotions, EDLP style, generally tends to attract slightly older and lower income groups in Asia, whereas high-low stores will capture a larger proportion of more affluent households. As a third point, the surveys we conducted show another attitude. Asian customers usually do not feel promotions have something to do with being loyal or disloyal to a store.

## Promotions and four customer profiles

At this point, you may want to address psychographics and try to see why Asian shoppers like promotions in general, and discounts in particular. Both Muslim and non-Muslim Asians seem to appreciate promotions more than foreigners. Do they like discounts because they feel that the customer is king and that a price cut is the way for a store to show respect? Is it because they like money and love calculating how much they save with each price rebate? Is it because they are poor and for them, even a few dollars will make a difference? Is it something else?

In fact what we have observed is that there are four customer groups when it comes to promotions. We call them **Triggers, Bank Account, Why-Pay-More,** and **Bargain Lovers.**

**Triggers** are approximately 10 percent of shoppers and tend to be upper-income customers. They can buy whatever they want relatively easily, within reason, when they see something attractive. It is because of them that we have a few more switchers in upscale department stores. For them a special offer is not just a price reduction but also a way to notice a product:

*"It's not only to save money, but I felt buying _____ when I saw the _____ being promoted."*

These shoppers are not buying everything they see on promotion of course, but a promotion will trigger their interest and as they feel they have a reasonably high disposable income, they tend to buy special offers.

The **Bank Account** group is at the other end of the spectrum. These customers also represent about 10 percent of shoppers, but, for them, saving a few dollars here and there is actually meaningful. They live on a budget and if they shop hypermarkets and department stores twice a month, and spend the equivalent of $30 each time, a theoretical 10 percent discount on all their purchase means they save nearly $150 per year.

*"I feel I have more money left when I buy a promotion."*

*"For me, the accumulated amount from many times of shopping will be big money."*

About 35 percent of the Asian shoppers belong to the **Why-Pay-More** profile. Their attitude is quite straightforward. If they need something and it is on special offer they are likely to buy and stock the product. The point for them is more rational than emotional. They simply don't see the point in paying a high price if they can avoid it

*"I simply feel I spend less money."*

*"Just a little money saving is OK."*

**Bargain Lovers,** the remaining group, is also the largest. They have the same income as the previous one, but their motivation is more emotional; there is a sense of achievement when selecting promoted items.

*" I feel happy to buy discount items."*

*" I'm proud to buy a discount product."*

Suzy, in Chapter 3, for example, is a Bargain Lover. When she decided to buy a set of two-for-one small fans, she actually had several ideas in mind. First, one of those could prove useful to her parents. Second, this promotion will last for a couple of weeks so if she comes back within the next ten days or so, she might buy another set of two-for-one electrical fans. It is more fun and more pleasurable to buy this promotion twice than if she bought two sets today. For her, it's twice the pleasure.

This attitude seems more common in countries that are still developing and to happen a bit less in emerging countries. In Asian developing markets, customers act more on a short term basis , not setting a budget limit for a shopping trip. If they have money today, they will spend today, purchasing the items promoted in multiples as long as they want these products with these designs. As Asian markets mature, some shoppers still make impulse purchases if they love a bargain, while others calculate their purchases in terms of budget and sequence.

The third point she had in mind was to see her husband's reaction and approval. If he'd say the plastic fans are cheap but he doesn't like them because they don't look good or any other reason, she'd answer this is for her parents as they need something like this and anyway, her parents don't care very much about the look. Incidentally, Suzy might still buy another set for her own household even if her husband doesn't like those, because he's now been exposed to them.

If the item were more expensive, a fourth point might apply. It is that she wouldn't want to spend too much money right away, even if she can afford it. If instead of small items, the promotion was for say, two-for-one pedestal electric fans with various cooling modes, and if she wanted two sets, i.e., four electric fans (which could very well happen), she would be reluctant to pay for the two sets right away. She would want to avoid the displeasure of spending a relatively high amount of money on the same day.

For a store in Asia, it is interesting to know that the Bargain Lovers tend to shop more frequently than other shoppers for fast moving consumer goods. As for the Why-Pay-Mores, they shop more often than others for personal needs, such as leisure and cultural products, as well as clothing. Knowing this, retailers can try to synchronize and adjust how long they should keep any kind of special event in their store, perhaps keeping the promotion a little longer than they planned originally.

# 7

# The Key Is Assortment

SO FAR we have addressed the shopper attitude and behavior toward an aspect of shopping convenience (location of a store) and toward money (price and promotions). But when people shop, it is in order to buy something, be it a service or a product, and we have to consider what they buy and why they go to a particular shop.

When we ask consumers in Asia why they shop at one store instead of another, the notion of choice comes up among the top two reasons. People use different words: selection, range, assortment, variety of products, or simply "many products," but in a nutshell, they refer to the possibility of finding what they need and want.

The specific answers to this question depend on the store type and the kind of product category we are probing. For several non-food categories, such as electronics or furniture, the quality of the products sold and the quality of delivery and installation are also important criteria. And for over-the-counter medicines, the important criteria relate to whether people believe that the products will be good for health, and whether they trust the professionalism of the staff members in the drugstore. But generally speaking, a large product range, a wide or deep selection, is critical for Asians to decide to shop a certain store.

## Assortment as criterion to select a store

For clothing and accessories, the variety of products that can be seen in a store is the top criterion, quite often for more than 60 percent of shoppers. For shops selling products like books, music, or movies on DVD, the selection is also key for 50 percent or more of the respondents.

Incidentally, this is also the case whether Asians buy genuine or counterfeit cultural products like pirated CDs or DVDs. In some Asian markets it is relatively easy to find a small booth on a sidewalk that displays color photocopies of original DVD covers. Looking at these jackets, customers just select the movie they want. For the pirate the whole process is very easy; all that's necessary is to display the titles. For the customers too, everything is quite easy. Once they decide on the titles they want, in a few minutes someone will bring the actual pirated DVD or CD in a mundane plastic bag. The transaction is done quickly and discretely. If the police come around, the small booth displaying the jackets is folded in a matter of seconds and there is no evidence of counterfeit because there is no actual pirated disc, just paper covers. So even for pirated cultural products, it is important to provide a large assortment.

If Asian shoppers want to buy technical products like telephones or computers, choice is also a major criterion when they decide which stores to visit. Assortment is not always the most important point, but it will be among the top two or three. For computers and IT in general, telephones and electric appliances, the variety of products available is important (at least 40 percent mention this as major criterion) and all major brands are expected to be displayed in a store. If an Asian family wants to buy a new TV set and they like Sony for instance, they want the store to sell the Sony brand, not just to have a great selection of TVs from other producers.

For home improvement and home interior, more than 50 percent will mention the variety of products among their top criteria as well but here, the brands will not be critical since brands are not strong in Asia for those items. We will come back with more details about what kind of choice the customers have in mind.

For fast moving consumer goods, assortment is also a major reason to select a store and is generally criterion number two or three. However, for hygiene/beauty and personal care, Asian shoppers are mostly females. For this category of products, the main decision factors are more related to price and promotions, as well as perceived quality and brand reputation, rather than choice. If a female shopper likes a certain cosmetic she will want to find it in the store where she goes and the fact that other brands and creams are available is nice to know but rarely of interest. This also means that more and more shoppers for personal care and beauty in Asia go to specialized stores. If they have a preferred brand and don't necessarily want to look at a huge selection of unwanted items, they will also want to be certain that they purchase a genuine product, not an imitation and not one that is close to the expiry date. As they are first degree, they may think that a specialized store is better equipped than a generalist in this regard. Even if both sell the same cosmetics at the same price, some customers will suspect a generalist keeps huge and outdated stocks. Even as they find their preferred brand in their usual store, they still appreciate a bargain and will look for promotions. Female Asian shoppers do not want to miss an opportunity to find the right product and the right deal, especially when they have the Bargain Lovers or the Bank Account profile.

For food items, Asian shoppers express needs that are different whether we refer to grocery or fresh produce and whether they are end-users or professionals. Individuals want a large selection for grocery, and this is the reason for the success of hypermarkets all over Asia. The large assortment for groceries that are available under one roof has been key (more than the low prices), for hypermarkets to capture customers away from the traditional markets. Perceived quality is generally not an issue as we saw, in the case of grocery and beverage.

At the modern trade outlets, some of the shoppers are not end-users but restaurant owners or caterers. These professionals shop at warehouse club outlets like Costco, Makro, or LotteMart Wholesale. They also shop for their businesses at some hypermarkets where they may represent a few percent of the sales turnover of those stores. For these professionals, too, the assortment of grocery is important, in particular for beverages, condiments, and canned foods, preferably for imported items and big packs. These caterers and restaurant operators pay attention to the choice of fresh food, especially in the case of fresh meat, fruits, and vegetables. Conversely mom-and-pop store owners, whether they sell grocery or fresh will not care very much about the large assortments they can find at modern trade outlets because they resell and their shops are small. They are simply offering a limited selection to their own customers.

For on-premise food, such as tablecloth restaurants and fast-food outlets, the end-users rank assortment as the number 3 criterion—less critical than quality or ease of access, but more important than price or proximity to home or to the workplace. About 40 percent of shoppers mention choice and the variety of products (dishes) available as their major criteria for choosing a restaurant.

All in all, it seems that whatever word we use—choice, selection, range, variety of products or variety of brands—the assortment is one of the top criteria when it comes to deciding where to shop. To see what kind of choice Asian shoppers are interested in, we have to distinguish what we call depth and width of assortment. In their own words, the customers talk about "stores with limited categories but big choice inside categories" versus "stores with many categories but less choice inside categories."

## Width and depth of assortment

In a store, a wide assortment is a selection of products addressing various needs. A deep assortment is a large choice of products for the same type of need. For example, if we consider a store offering sports shoes we can look at what sports are covered or what needs are fulfilled. The width of assortment in this case would correspond to different kinds of shoes based on different sports such as footwear for basketball, soccer, jogging, and so forth. Each sport can be considered as one specific need, since you will not play a sport like badminton with soccer shoes.

On the other hand the assortment depth refers to one specific need, in this case one sport, such as basketball. For basketball shoes the depth of assortment will involve variations on the theme. You will have basketball shoes with different midsoles and outsoles, different ankle collars, or hidden shoelaces, not to mention styles for males and for females, various colors and sizes, and of course the various brands. If a market is developed and segmented, customers are conscious of having specific needs and the assortment depth becomes relevant as customers want a specific pair of sport shoes for a specific need.

In Asia, whether or not the market is developed and segmented, the depth of assortment is always relevant. It can be relevant because of rational needs. Let's continue with the sport shoes example. If baseball is popular as in Korea and Japan, or if basketball is a major sport as in the Philippines, there will be good reasons for a store to provide a deep assortment because various customers may really have specific needs. But the depth of assortment is important even if it does not address a real purpose. One reason is face. Asian customers want to be able to show to others that they have something unique. In a sporting goods store selling golf clubs, even an inexperienced shopper can buy the latest, and largest, Big Bertha driver. It may not be because it is particularly user friendly or because of the material such as titanium or graphite, but very possibly due to the head size—the part that actually hits the ball can have a maximum volume of $460 \, cm^3$ and for many Asian customers, the bigger the product, the better. In a store selling mobile phones and accessories, shoppers will want a PDA or the iPad 2 that is either the newest one in town or slightly different than usual, with an uncommon casing, a different color, or a specific feature. To cater with these needs and wants, the stores in Asia have to offer depth of assortment.

Another reason is creativity or, what is often considered as a lack of personal creativity among Asian customers. A shopper wants to own something unique but at the same time, will tend to be a follower in terms of fashion or trendiness, so Asian shoppers need stores to inspire them. The desire to buy sport shoes is just a starting point. To convert the visitor into an actual shopper, a store will need to showcase various kinds of sneakers in various sporting situations. The shopper will look around and find the item that looks inspiring and different.

A shopper in Asia buying something for home improvement—tiles to renovate the bathroom for instance—will also need depth of assortment. He will go to a home improvement store, or to the local, traditional market for materials and look for tiles. What will be important to him will be the perceived quality of the tiles and prices, of course, but the critical issue will be styles. What are the various materials, shapes, colors, patterns, and designs? If a DIY store displays a large array of tiles in this case, it is likely that the customer will pick one. And the better the store is at showcasing these materials, the more likely the shopper is to buy. It is not just a question of price. If the store displays a complete bathroom, showing the end result, the shopper can visualize what his bathroom could look like and when it gives ideas and stimulation to the shopper it is even better.

Here are some verbatims from Asian shoppers that illustrate this need for a deep assortment.

*"What I am looking for is unique designs."*     (female, late twenties)

*"I need new ideas; after visiting [the store] I didn't get any idea."*

(male, 38)

*"I wish to find more selection and styles in this store."*  (female, 34)

If we express this in terms of percentage, the desire for a deep assortment is very clear. Nearly 70 percent, both male and female, will prefer "limited categories with large choice inside categories," There is virtually no variance based on income groups, average age, or education levels. This is actually not good news for generalists if they think of saturating a market with small or medium size outlets. Department stores, hypermarket chains, and some category killers may be tempted to open a large number of compact stores so as to be "present everywhere" with stores requiring a relatively low investment because the format is smaller than usual. It is likely to be a problem though, whenever these outlets stock up products for multiple basic needs (wide offer) but with little depth; potential customers will be frustrated.

What shoppers are talking about is not simply to have a large choice for the pleasure of seeing a big range of products. They actually need to see a deep assortment in order to be inspired. They want to find products that stand out, that will be as unique as possible, and in return, will make them feel unique.

It would be easy to conclude that Asians want to buy something with a special design because this will reflect on them positively, because they expect they'll be admired and thus gain face. After all, if you own the latest product of any kind, be it the newest running shoes or the latest Tablet and if this can be seen by others, you do gain face in the Far East. One can arguably say that the main motivation for any Asian shopper is to be perceived as an up-to-date person. In fact, the motivation is perhaps not purely and not only face. In a way we could say Asian shoppers are bored easily with the products they buy and are constantly looking for novelties when it comes to shopping. This is comparable to a short attention span.

## Show me something new

When an Asian shopper buys equipment or virtually any non-food item, he or she will think something like this:

*"I don't care too much about the quality because after a few years or a few months, I'll be tired of it and will want to replace it."*

This applies more or less to any durable product, a dress or a jacket, a sofa or another piece of furniture, a new TV set or a small electric appliance.

Looking for novelties will also be the case for food items such as general groceries or most of the packaged goods category. For food and even for personal care, 40 percent of shoppers consider assortment as a major criterion to select a store. Among these 40 percent, a large share say that what they have in mind with assortment, is actually "new products." This is not just about face. You don't "impress the Jones" because you bought the new breakfast cereals or the latest squid-flavored noodle soup. The motivation here is to try something new for the sake of it. It is new both in terms of expiry date, of course, but also in terms of originality or innovation. It can revive the interest in the product category.

This motivation puts in perspective the concept of one-stop-shopping. The idea behind this concept is that the assortment will not be deep; it only has to be wide. You go to a one-stop-shop and you can find one or two products for each of your possible needs—a few kinds of noodle packs or a few mobile phones in a hypermarket, a few treadmills at a sporting goods store, or a few tiles at a category killer that is more a generalist than a specialist. The one-stop-shop saves time. You don't need to go to many different stores to fulfill your basic needs, but for each of these customer needs you will not find many items to chose from. In Asia, the point is that many shoppers actually love to run around and go to various outlets. It is not simply in order to fulfill a need. Comparing products and prices, of course, and browsing can be a kind of hobby.

One-stop-shopping can work very well in Asia for mundane products like groceries at hypermarkets, because most of these are fast moving items. If Asians want to buy cooking oil, rice, and ice cream it makes sense for them to buy those at a hypermarket because they are quite sure they will find the top brands and the shoppers generally buy their usual brand without thinking much about it. Whenever a producer puts a new item on the market, it will be promptly available at the hypermarket or the supermarket, so the need to have the latest product can also be met.

However, one-stop-shopping is more of a challenge for category killers: a toy store, a sporting goods retailer, a home interior specialist, or a large bookstore must not only address all kinds of needs, it must also display an assortment that is deep enough for each of the needs. Otherwise shoppers are likely to browse around, feel like the choice is actually not that impressive, leave without buying anything, and may not come back. There are two solutions for category killers in the Far East other than to compete on prices (and potentially lose money): either differentiate with a deep selection for at least some of the product categories that they sell, and provide a certain number of those unique and new designs that Asian people are looking for, or obtain some kind of endorsement from local opinion leaders for their current product category.

A sporting goods store in Asia can be successful because of its deep assortment of athletic footwear and up-to-date golf clubs, despite a weaker selection on other sports equipment. A toy specialist can thrive because its chain stores have the latest educational toys, even if they don't have a wide range for dolls and action figures. Well known opinion leaders endorsing a sporting goods chain could mean that golf and sport instructors recommend that chain or would advertise for it. Local teachers may also endorse a toy store focusing on edutainment or toys with some educational value. For a home improvement retailer with low visibility, an endorsement could convince local contractors and designers to recommend the chain to end-users, when these individuals need professional assistance as they remodel their homes.

There is a limit to the efficiency of backing by opinion leaders. In the end it is likely that depth in the product range will be necessary anyway, because the professionals who endorse the retailers also want to remain credible; they don't simply want a fee. They may recommend the chain if, in the eye of the end user, there is a good reason, and if this good reason is visible. At least part of the assortment must have great style, good design, or something that can be perceived as new or unique. In other words the depth of assortment is still a pre-requisite.

## There are many kinds of shopping malls downtown

If the assortment challenge for retailers in Asia is to touch the imagination and trigger the interest of shoppers, the good news is that a store will benefit from the assortment of its neighbors, even if it has a small sales area because a line-up of small independent stores, if seen together, in effect displays a large offering. A shopping mall concept may have difficulty succeeding in Asia if shoppers don't want to go to a giant commercial center on a regular basis when they can still find a large array of small shops downtown. These stores play the same role for them as a shopping mall.

A city like Taipei, for instance, is arguably a large shopping mall in itself. Streets are filled with fashion retailers, shops that sell accessories, technical products, and affordable on-premise or take-away food. If shoppers in Taipei mostly need to "see" several products in order to be inspired, it makes sense for them to visit and browse all those small stores. The shops don't necessarily offer the latest international fashion, but shoppers who look for clothes do not follow the international fashion that much anyway. What the shopper wants is to look at all the various shops and not miss a single one, especially women, because they don't want to take the risk of missing a unique product that they might find in one of those small outlets. If the customer needs technical products, the situation is the same. Shoppers who want some electronic goods, for instance, will go to the special district in town where dozens of small retailers offer mobile phones, computers, and various electronic goods. By visiting all or most of those outlets, shoppers will find inspiration and the right products for them. If you have one product family in mind, and you want to review all the possible offers in town, it makes sense to go to the district that specializes in that category.

In Asian cities, when we probe the various types of satisfaction and dissatisfaction at shopping malls and department stores the usual finding is that customers will say they are quite happy, More than 60 percent are either very or at least somewhat satisfied with their overall shopping experience in a given mall. In a nutshell, customers visiting a shopping mall or a department store in Asia are happy with the quality of merchandise and the shopping environment, but not really thrilled by the staff competence, nor by the prices (but they accept the price points). In terms of choice the satisfaction rates okay.

While assortment only provides an "okay satisfaction" overall, there is a difference between the judgment about variety of products and brands on the one hand, and satisfaction about modernity of those products on the other hand. Product variety, and brand variety are perceived as good at modern trade outlets generally. Asian shoppers recognize that in a department store or in a shopping mall, there are 150,000 SKUs (stock keeping units) or more and there is a wide and deep choice. But modernity is the attribute that rates constantly lower. If we probe a little further about the meaning of "modernity" for the Asian customers, the response is that it means:

- new arrival
- new products
- in-trend items
- new technology

From a different angle, if we ask a question such as "what are the strong points and the weak points" of the department store or the shopping mall, we get similar feedback. The customers talk mostly about assortment, variety of products, and modern, up-to-date merchandise. Whether it is for a positive or negative view, their comments relate more to the choice and selection than to proximity to home or any other issue. If we ask open questions another way, "What should the department store (or the shopping mall) do to improve?" and let customers answer whatever they want, we have more answers about new products or the latest fashion than comments about the in-store decoration, the service, or the value for money. Here again, the underlying request is not so much to have fancy lighting or an innovative store layout; it is not even just to see "a lot of stuff." The key point about products is about finding novelties.

Therefore, if a mall doesn't address this motivation very well, such as just having an "okay rating" about product modernity, the shopping mall will suffer from competition by the small stores downtown, even if these are not trendy or stylish themselves, and even if they don't offer a great shopping environment. Shoppers in Asia want unique things, and if they feel there is a good chance to find those in the multiple small outlets downtown, they will dedicate a good share of their time and budget to these small stores. The downtown shops that are grouped in part of the city, for all intents and purposes, are a shopping mall.

The word "mall" in Asia covers different formats. It generally stands for large commercial centers of 100,000 or more square meters, with several anchors (food retailer operating several thousand square meters, big-box category killers) and multiple small outlets. However, in Asian cities, the word mall is also used to describe the dozen small shops or so that are attached to a hypermarket. These are generally tenants of the hypermarket company and benefit from the traffic generated by the large food retailer. Instead of *mall*, internally we prefer to use the term *shopping gallery* when we refer to the limited number of small shops attached to the hypermarket. Their combined sales area can reach a thousand square meters or larger in the case when a category killer or two is also established in the same building. The category killer can be a furniture store, a toy retailer, a technical goods specialist, or a cultural goods and book store and is generally called co-anchor. Such a mall is sometimes referred to as power center.

For the company that operates the mall or the power center (often it is the hypermarket chain), these tenants are a very good source of revenue. The reason for having a series of co-anchors and small stores as well as a food court is rarely subject to debate. These outlets not only help attract customers, but they also pay rent and provide a significant source of income to the operator. Financially this is a win-win arrangement because, in return, the hypermarket generates most of the foot traffic.

In terms of marketing, it makes sense for the management of the hypermarket to ensure that its tenants complement the offer. The assortment has to be somewhat different. In other words the small shops need to be relevant toward the households who live in the geographic zone, yet, should not have an offer that competes directly with the hypermarket. One way for hypermarkets to differentiate is to provide brands that belong exclusively to their chains.

## Store brands and private labels

The concept of store brands, also called private labels, house brands, or national brand equivalents, is interesting. On the one hand, those items are solely available at a specific retail chain: Carrefour products, Tesco products, Walmart's Great Value, B&Q ECO, and Kirkland at Costco outlets, for example. Some are specially designed by the chain and qualify as unique products.

On the other hand, Asian customers are brand-conscious. They are not just fond of luxury goods; they like a product with a brand name, whether for chocolate cookies, shampoo, or mineral water. If this is the case, are they going to appreciate private labels if those have no premium image?

To see what happens, in the case of store brands, let's compare two middle-class households doing their shopping at a supercenter, one in a Western country, one in Asia. In their stores, both families will buy fresh produce, maybe some books or household utensils, and surely they will buy a significant quantity of packaged goods. For reference, at a typical hypermarket, groceries and personal care items will represent around 40 percent of the average ticket in the West, but over 60-65 percent of the average basket in Asia. The difference is due to fresh food, which represents about 30 percent of the basket in the West but around 10 percent in the Far East in terms of expenditure.

For groceries, both families will have a large assortment to choose from, which includes national and international brands, at certain price points. We can take the example of yogurt and consider they find a pack of 500 gram Nestle strawberry yogurt at the price of 100. In a Tesco store, this family can also select a 500 gram pack of Tesco strawberry yogurt; the same can be said with Carrefour or Walmart. The Tesco yogurt here is the house brand and its price will be around 80, a good 20 percent cheaper than the international brand. The shoppers can probably find an even cheaper strawberry yogurt as well, with another brand name (let's say brand X) sold at 65, or 35 percent cheaper than the well-known brand. This lower tier is the entry price for that particular product— strawberry yogurt. In Asia it is often called First Price. Roughly speaking, about 10 percent of the sales at hypermarkets in Asia belong to the house brand/First Price group of products. Those are cheap but actually more profitable for the retail chain than international brands are, because the retailer is the one managing the production. But other than profitability, the underlying idea for the chain is also to differentiate. Retailers know that they all offer essentially the same packaged goods as far as national and international brands are concerned, at comparable prices. So more and more the chains want to provide some different products with slightly different taste, composition, texture, etc. From the retailer's point of view the house brand has the same quality as the comparable international brand but it is cheaper with a better margin.

From the shopper's point of view, the house brand is a good idea too. Customers have been told that the reason it is cheaper is because the chain saves on the marketing cost. If the house brand yogurt is not advertised on TV or newspapers, the money saved goes back to the customer through a lower price. This is a powerful, logical, convincing idea. It is rational. For the First Price a slightly different thought applies. In addition to saving on the cost of advertising, the quality is marginally lower. The taste can still be acceptable but the overall quality may be inferior to the international brands or the house brand. The trade-off for customers is that they save more money, and for many mundane or basic items, they happily accept First Price brands. After all, consumers may think a tissue paper is a tissue paper, a can of sardines is just sardines.

In Asia, shoppers do not really understand the difference between a house brand and a First Price item. The confusion is partly because of communication but also due to the small number of items involved. With groceries, while Carrefour or Tesco would display more than two thousand SKUs of house brand items in Europe, they have a few hundred in Asia. Since exposure is low, shoppers have little chance to really purchase private labels and little chance to try both kinds, the house brand and the First Price.

The use and purchase of store brands varies depending on the business the retailer covers. At hypermarkets and supercenters, the ratio of shoppers who say they purchase house brands can range anywhere from 20 to 70 percent. This is a huge variance but it does not depend on the country; the purchase of store brands depends on the chain itself. At many hypermarkets in Asia, only half of the shoppers know that there are store brands or private labels in the first place; the other half may buy those without knowing they are house brands. When such a low awareness occurs, essentially it means the hypermarket did not make it well known.

At other hypermarket chains about 90 percent of customers actually know there are some sorts of private label products. The second reason for the huge variance is whether customers are willing to purchase at least some of the store brand items. In fact, it appears Asian customers are willing to buy pretty much any commodity under the store brand as long as they believe the chain is a "good" company. Saying that Asians feel a hypermarket cannot possibly offer good quality items under its store-brand *because* a hypermarket is a generalist would be wrong. Asian shoppers know very well that hypermarkets are not specialists, but, if a retailer is serious about its store brands and manages a large assortment with good quality, Asian shoppers will recognize that and the satisfaction levels in terms of choice and perceived quality can be good, even when customers talk about the private labels.

Conversely, a hypermarket chain with a weak general image will also have weak ratings on its house brands. Shoppers will only say the price is low, nothing more, and will claim those products have low quality as well, with potentially other claims such as the private labels are not that cheap after all, not famous, and so forth. They will have comments such as:

> ". . . the paper cups that have the store's brand name may cost less than the famous brand ones, but each time, I have to use two instead of one, so actually it costs more."

Asian customers can accept and appreciate store brands, when the retailer takes its line of products seriously and vice versa. We think there is no cultural or mental block. There is only a perception that the customer is respected and offered good quality products or is not.

There is a flip side about store brands, the same as in the West. Even when retailers truly respect the shoppers and provide good quality, shoppers don't really differentiate house brands. An Asian shopper, just like an American or a European shopper, will simply love the *concept* of private label (same quality, 20 percent cheaper) and will gladly buy those at any hypermarket. A Tesco strawberry yogurt is not perceived so different from a Carrefour strawberry yogurt.

There can be exceptions when a category killer is perceived as a specialist. The health and beauty chain Watsons, with stores in Korea, Greater China, and several Southeast Asian countries, is often considered as a personal care specialist. Its shoppers are overwhelmingly women (nearly 80 percent) and they are young, with nearly half under age 25, and often students. For them toiletries and cosmetics are sensitive and emotional purchases. About half of these shoppers buy personal care items with the Watsons brand name on it, such as make-up accessories, moisturizers, wet tissues, dental accessories, or bath foam. They feel it is safe to buy the house brand because they consider the chain is an expert in its field.

For non-food retailers, house brands also exist in Asia and represent only 10 percent of sales or less. An appliance chain can sell national brands but also have two or three store brands for some electronics such as monitors, or for some small appliance like toasters or juice squeezers. The shoppers are predominantly male (more than 60 percent) although they sometimes go to the store with their wives or children. When asked whether they ever bought the retailer's store brands, only 10 to 12 percent of the customers say they have, while 60 to 65 percent answer no. The remaining are not sure, and we cannot blame them because at category killers, the store brands often have a different name than the chain. A shopper at a Tsann Kuen appliance store (a chain having difficulty on the Chinese market) doesn't know if the Eupa brand belongs to the chain or not. At Toys'R'Us, a customer who buys a Steffi doll may or may not think this is a Toys'R'Us house brand. In a Chinese outlet of B&Q home improvement products, a shopper looking at the long shelves of paint with the brand B&Q Eco and B&Q Value might think:

*"Oh, this must be a huge company, they own stores and they also own so many paint factories, to produce all these buckets . . ."*

## For minorities too, the key is assortment

Some minorities in the Far East are represented only in a few places, such as the aboriginals in Taiwan, or can be considered only as an approximate benchmark, such as the foreigners who shop in Asia. But others, like the Muslims are present in many countries as we pointed out earlier.

Regarding assortment, specific groups like aboriginals tend to care as much as other residents about the variety of brands and even slightly more than others about the variety of products.

Foreign shoppers tend to be more satisfied than Asians with the selection they find in stores. Where 25 percent of foreigners say they are satisfied with the variety of brands and 40 percent are satisfied with the variety of products, Asian customers in the same store will show only 20 percent and 30 percent satisfaction ratings respectively. The same is true for the appreciation of modern or up-to-date products—35 percent for foreigners versus 25 percent for Asians. Customers in the Far East tend to be less easily satisfied, and more demanding about assortment than Westerners.

The comparison between Asian Muslims and non-Muslims shows that in both of these groups, the customers consider assortment as a major criterion, with little variance. It is only for consumer electronics and big appliances perhaps, that Muslims appear even more sensitive to choice than other Asians. This could be due to income since Muslim households are less well-off on average and may require a larger selection for expensive items like refrigerators, washing machines, or TVs, in the hope to find more choice at an entry price level.

Irrespective of a minority group or a country's level of development though, we think one reason why Asian customers want to see a large array of products is because they need to see the real items in a store in order to be inspired. Another reason is that their parents and grandparents never experienced abundance. Asian shoppers of today want to enjoy all the merchandise they can get and that the previous generation could not afford. The older generations did benefit from one thing however, the cultural notion of service. This is addressed in the next chapter.

# 8

# Service: Facilities and Staff

A SHOPPER experiences two different kinds of service. Broadly speaking, those either relate to facilities or to staff members. A parking lot, the store cleanliness, the trolleys, or the overall store environment are all facilities issues. Whether you feel welcome, whether you have quick and correct answers to your questions depends on the store staff. Of course a clean store means janitors do a good job and a cashier will be friendlier if enough checkout counters are open and if the cashier is not overwhelmed. Services based on facilities and services from staff are inter-related, but we think it is useful to distinguish both sets of attributes.

## Facilities: entering a store

Aside from advertisements, the first contact with the store is often the parking lot. The parking facility is perhaps the single most underestimated aspect of a store. Many retail professionals do not think of the parking arrangement as a point of contact with their customers. Many others feel this space should be allocated to additional vendors. They think it is very smart to take 500 square meters off the parking space and rent it out to generate additional revenue, but by doing so they often forget that regular customers need to park their cars. They also forget that if customers experience difficulty parking their vehicle two or three times in a row, they may decide not to come back to the particular store or shopping mall.

Having said that, Asian shoppers' satisfaction about parking lots is generally good, with about 70 percent expressing satisfaction (a little less than that in Taiwan or Singapore, a little more in Korea or Thailand). The remaining 30 percent experience some frustration.

In Korea and Japan the dissatisfaction is not about the overall size of the parking lot. Customers have cars; retailers know this and there is usually enough space for all the vehicles. In Korea there are sometimes one or two levels of a parking facility dedicated to female drivers—the alleys are wider, the lighting is brighter, and the parking area is larger than at the other floors. The reason is that females in Korea are not considered good drivers. This is the consensus among male Koreans but many Korean ladies agree. Therefore, if a Korean retailer facilitates the driving conditions within a parking lot for the female customers, the accommodation is appreciated.

In markets like Korea and Japan, the dissatisfaction about parking lots concerns the difficulty of getting in or out. Because space is rare and expensive, many retailers in these countries try to save a few square meters by constructing a relatively narrow ramp where cars drive into and exit the parking facility. Drivers have a difficult time entering some malls, and part of their judgment about how well customers are treated is already made before they put one foot in the stores, based on how easy or difficult it has been to drive into the car park.

In Chinese markets, the experience with parking depends on the level of income and particularly the proportion of shoppers who own a vehicle. In Mainland China, even though more and more people have a car, a large ratio of customers go to their shopping destinations by bus. On average, about 40 percent of shoppers at a shopping mall that has a hypermarket as main anchor go there by bus while another 30 percent go either by foot or bicycle. When a shopper comes by bicycle, it will not necessarily mean he or she does not own a car. It may be that the shoppers know they are likely to be unable to park. In effect, when we ask about satisfaction with the parking arrangements, we often have more negative answers from shoppers who came by bicycle with the negative response being typically about the insufficient number of places for cars. In richer Chinese markets like Singapore and Taiwan, the ratio of shoppers coming by car is around 45 percent for shopping destinations anchored by a hypermarket. In Taiwan, the other means of transportation is motorbike (around 40 percent of shoppers), while in Singapore shoppers also come by public transport including subway and bus. The satisfaction with parking arrangements is not very high, only around 60 percent and the issue is also an insufficient number of places.

With Southeast Asian markets that are not Chinese, like Malaysia or Thailand, the proportion of shoppers who drive to the mall is high at above 60 percent. The parking facilities tend to be large and visitors are generally satisfied with the parking lot. Dissatisfactions are minor, still due to the limited number of places for the cars (very few complaints about dirtiness, lack of light or feelings of insecurity). Less developed countries like Cambodia, Vietnam, or Indonesia still show a limited, yet increasing, level of car users and the situation there is a bit similar to that of China. A small number of bays for cars will tend to induce low satisfaction about the car park and will not encourage shoppers to drive to the stores, even if they own a car.

## Shopping environment

Once the vehicle is parked, the customers enter the commercial outlet and generally walk through the ground floor (F1). As we saw earlier, this floor is often dedicated to a shopping gallery, 15 to 30 shops selling mostly non-food items that do not directly compete with the main anchor.

Once the shoppers pass through F1, using the travelator, they reach the hypermarket, which is the main destination, one floor up. In some cases, hypermarkets offer an escalator. With a shopping cart however you cannot use the escalator easily. With a travelator you can bring your trolley from floor to floor.

The shopping environment is also about the ease of movement inside the mall and the main store. Satisfaction on this attribute is generally above 75 percent in most Asian countries and often above 80 percent. The small complaints refer to cartons and pallets that are sometimes scattered in the aisles at the time when employees refill the shelves. It makes walking along the gondolas a little uneasy, but customers accept this if they see the staff working. Conversely they will complain if they see a skid with nobody attending it for more than a minute or so.

However, the main point about the overall shopping environment does not relate so much to the shopping gallery or walking around in-store. It is more an issue of ambiance and atmosphere at the main anchor store. The satisfaction here is generally quite consistent in all Asian markets for comparable types of stores; it varies, not according to countries, but to store formats. If a large store is crowded, visitors feel that moving around is not easy. They accept this if they feel it is because the store is successful, but not if they consider the walking aisles are too narrow.

Generally speaking customers in the Far East want to have space in a store. Whereas in the West many shoppers would say they appreciate boutique malls or "human-size" shopping destinations as opposed to very large outlets, most of the time in Asia we see more than 50 percent preferring a "big shopping mall." Less than 10 percent have an opposite opinion. For retailers in Asia, especially in the case of food retail, the ambiance and environment in store was not always a priority in the past because other points had greater importance. Many Asian retailers would primarily want to facilitate traffic:

*"What's important is to have shoppers come in, buy as much as possible quickly, and go back home."*

(Thailand, manager of supermarket)

For other retailers the priority is merchandise:

*"I don't care too much if my stores feel less nice than others; as long as I offer better prices."*          (Korea, manager of hypermarket)

Today, store chains neglect this less and less and are more willing to offer a pleasant experience, not just in developed Asian countries but also in the emerging economies. In rather developed markets like Taiwan and Hong Kong, more than 25 percent of the shoppers will spontaneously mention the overall ambiance as one of their criteria to select a shopping destination; sometimes a higher percentage in the case of non-food. If a new shopping mall is to open, these potential customers consider whether it will provide "enjoyable shopping experience," and not simply a good level of comfort or safety.

In less developed territories, customers are still less sensitive to the overall atmosphere the percentage is around 10 percent, but it is increasing. Currently, shoppers in emerging markets pay attention to a store's room temperature—for them modern trade means air conditioning, not fixed prices. In the decade 2011–2020 it is likely that even in emerging countries, new malls will provide more than products, air conditioning, and walking space. They will display "lifestyle outlets" with fashion stores, upscale coffee shops, bookstores, trendy bakeries, and entertainment zones. Food and beverage outlets, for instance, appear as a new phenomenon in countries like Indonesia as the incomes for individuals have been growing by around 8 percent yearly.

Other than the entertainment aspects, the ambiance of a retail establishment in Asia also stems from the overall look of the store—the appearance of the shopping environment. Currently shoppers appear generally satisfied with the environment because they are ambivalent about this. They like a product display that looks modern and sophisticated, but they also appreciate a less organized store, where you have to search for the products because a store that looks a little messy (as long as it's reasonably clean) is considered inexpensive. In both cases, the environment and atmosphere can be considered good. Organized store layouts are more appreciated in developed economies and when shoppers have a higher education level.

Most category killers show high ratings on their store environment in most Asian markets (home improvement chains, appliance specialists, furniture stores), generally 85 percent satisfaction or above, and the same can be said for department stores. Formats where the shopping environment is a bit less satisfactory (but still around 75 percent) seem to be medium size, for both food outlets like supermarkets, and non-food, sporting goods for instance—stores where aisles are not wide, but where a large array of products can be found. To summarize, in virtually all countries, Asian shoppers who are in their thirties or younger, feel the overall ambiance at modern trade outlets is far superior to the shopping environment at traditional markets.

What is important for a retailer is a shopping environment that makes a customer feel like staying longer—the longer a shopper stays in a store, the more he or she is likely to spend. Customers typically stay 45 to 55 minutes, but shoppers who stay more than one hour will spend about 35 percent more than the average. Conversely, for those who shop only 30 minutes, the expenditure will be about 20 percent less than average. It would be too easy to conclude that those who buy more have to "mechanically" stay longer. If the ambiance and the shopping environment successfully encourage shoppers to stay an additional fifteen minutes, there is an indirect effect on the average ticket; it's not just the other way round.

## Trolleys or shopping carts

In stores where customers need a basket or a shopping cart, such as hypermarkets, supermarkets and some category killers, the trolley is an integral part of the shopping experience, and retailers should probe this. In all Asian markets, when we measure customer satisfaction about trolleys, we generally find similar results: no particular variance by countries, but simply results based on common sense.

In Japan, the satisfaction levels on trolleys at shopping malls and hypermarkets are often very low, on the order of 55 percent (55 percent is not good). Any topic where only about one half of the customers are satisfied requires attention. When Japanese shoppers are not satisfied with trolleys, it is generally because those are too big. A Japanese female is slight and shops frequently. She buys a few items each time. And, her home is not large—less than 50 or 60 square meters per household in urban areas—with a small refrigerator and storage cabinets. In a general merchandise store, she has little need for a 150 liter shopping trolley.

In Chinese markets, most retail food shoppers are also women, but their satisfaction with shopping carts is above 70 percent in China, above 80 percent in Taiwan, and reaches 90 percent in Singapore. The causes for dissatisfaction reflect the sophistication of the markets. Trolleys "run badly" in China because of lack of maintenance and trolleys are "too big" in Singapore (but in good condition), similar to Japan.

In non-Chinese Southeast Asia the satisfaction about shopping carts is about 85 percent. When shoppers are offered the choice between a trolley and a basket, they select what corresponds to their needs at the moment, i.e., a basket if they plan to buy a limited quantity of products. Satisfaction about baskets is slightly higher than with trolleys. Baskets require less maintenance. They don't have a coin locker system that can break. They don't have wheels that squeak or get blocked.

However, causes for dissatisfaction still exist. There are more complaints about baskets being too small than too big. Baskets may be dirty: a decayed piece of vegetable or a torn piece of paper at the bottom of a basket reflects on the chain's image (but not too much), or baskets are damaged. The third issue may come as a surprise—baskets are not easy to find. This comment appears less and less however. In the past Asian store directors were afraid that sales would drop if customers didn't use large trolleys and were a little reluctant to prominently display baskets. Today, they think more in terms of shopping convenience and baskets are placed at different points of the store and at the entrance where they are easy to find.

## Locating products

Is it generally easy or difficult for Asian customers to find the products they came for?

In Japan and Korea, shoppers are not easily satisfied about this. One issue is the visibility of in-store signage. Signs can be half hidden by promotional displays, placed too high, or hard to read for some reason. Sometimes the reason can be as simple as the sign background being too dark or the typeface being too small. In all those cases, the Japanese and

Korean customers feel uncomfortable in store. Another issue is due to the height of a typical gondola. But the main issue we have encountered is about the remodeling of a store or changing part of the merchandising plan. Customers, especially in Japan, dislike when their products are not placed in the usual order. The "usual order" here has two meanings: first "as it used to be in this store." Japanese shoppers don't like to see too much change, so if a store manager decides to relocate some product categories like placing diapers near the baby food section while diapers used to be near the tissue department, shoppers will not feel good about it. There is a second meaning: "as it's usually done at other stores," in which case the shoppers say they don't want an outlet to have a shelf layout that would be too surprising.

In Chinese markets, customers have fewer problems with locating products. The satisfaction on this is often above 80 percent. When there is dissatisfaction, it's mostly due to logistic problems, such as product shortages or when the aisles are too crowded; for instance, in China we often see a very large number of shoppers at cosmetics aisles. The complaint about departments being moved is less prominent than in Japan.

As Chinese customers are sensitive to promotions, the main issue about locating products relates to the link between leaflets placed in mailboxes and the promoted items in the stores. If shoppers see an interesting special offer in a brochure at home they expect to find the promoted items in the store. The challenge is not only to avoid shortages; it is to facilitate finding the items on promotion. It's a question of in-store signage, guiding shoppers to all the promotions seen in the brochure. It's also a question of training the employees. All too often, customers complain that the store employees were unable to tell them where to find a particular item seen in the leaflet.

The same occurs in Southeast Asia, were shoppers almost always feel the products are easy to find (80 percent satisfaction or more) but note that the staff members in store are not very knowledgeable about the location of specific merchandise.

If we look across store formats, there are some major differences.

Department stores generally achieve the highest ratings (90 percent satisfaction on the ease of finding products) but for category killers it varies widely by country and product specialty (from 45 percent to 90 percent satisfaction in finding products). The challenge is particularly acute for books and stationery stores as it is often difficult for a customer to find the exact writing materials or the cultural product they would like to buy.

## Locating prices

Another aspect of shopping convenience, which is often overlooked, is about the price tags. Are price labels clear and legible? Is it easy for shoppers to see and know accurately the price of an item in a modern trade outlet? We can address this issue only for modern trade because by definition, traditional markets do not display their prices (as mentioned, the distinction between modern trade and traditional is whether prices are set and are the same for all, or whether you can haggle and negotiate).

In northeast Asia, shoppers are not too pleased, but don't complain too much either, regarding the price tags. In Japan and Korea ratings of 70 percent or 75 percent satisfaction for this are common. When there is dissatisfaction, it is generally because the price labels are missing, the price from the bar code at the time of payment does not correspond with the price tag, or the price label is not easy to read. Since older people have more difficulty reading small print, retailers in aging societies like Japan and China need to pay attention to price labels' legibility. The other issue with price tags is that shoppers in Korea and Japan are sensitive to the quality of the label itself, not in terms of thickness of the paper or the brightness of the colors used for printing, but in terms of the information displayed. The labels must be complete, with all relevant information to avoid the risk of misunderstanding, and they must be placed perfectly in line with the product. We observed this need in Japan and Korea more than in other Asian countries. Here again, in markets other than Japan and Korea, the shoppers tend to be more satisfied about shopping convenience. Ratings often reach more than 80 to 85 percent satisfaction for the ease in locating prices. The difference of satisfaction is significant (satisfaction of around 70 percent in Japan Korea, but around 85 percent in the rest of Asia).

This has to do with the expectation of the shopper, not just the actual location of the price labels. Chinese and Southeast Asian shoppers are less picky about price tags. Of course, they need the price to be indicated and to be fairly legible. They also expect that the price written on the label will be the same as what they pay once at the checkout counter but if a price label is not complete, or is badly placed along the shelves, it is not *that* serious and they feel they can understand what price tag goes with what product. They connect the dots, as it were.

## Cleanliness and resting areas

Cleanliness is perhaps the first of the services a store has to offer. As far as modern trade is concerned, stores are perceived clean generally in all Asian markets. There is a minor variance as the satisfaction on this attribute ranges between 85 to 95 percent. The difference on perceived cleanliness is partly related to the wealth of the countries and their level of development but also depends on the attention paid to cleanliness from a cultural standpoint.

A chain having a similar concept across Asia will typically obtain high ratings in every country. In Japan, the score will show that 95 percent or more of the shoppers are completely satisfied with cleanliness. In Korea it will be 90 percent. In a country like Thailand, the satisfaction level will reach 95 percent on cleanliness. The same retail brand will show a little more than 85 percent satisfaction on cleanliness in developed Chinese markets like Taiwan or Singapore but only 80 percent in its Mainland China stores.

For a traditional retailer, not a wet market but a local store in a Chinese country or in Southeast Asia, cleanliness appears in a totally different light. In a food outlet belonging to a local chain, cleanliness ratings are very low and we have more shoppers saying negative comments than positive ones. These ratings could be interpreted as a weakness. If nearly two thirds of the shoppers feel the cleanliness is a weak point of the retail outlet, this underscores a major problem that has to be tackled right away. However we must also recognize that, in Chinese countries in particular, the cleanliness drawback is not considered as an extremely strong issue and some lack of cleanliness, combined with a messy layout and old-fashioned looking fixtures can provide a good price image. If it looks lousy, it's probably cheap when seeing is believing. However, the lack of cleanliness must stay within reasonable limits. A store cannot be overly dirty; spilled milk cannot be decaying along the gondolas; old and dirty cartons should not be visible in a category killer store. But a wet area near the fish section of a supermarket, disorganized shelf space on old-looking gondolas, pallets scattered along the shopper's path in a local store may be perceived as a slight lack of cleanliness, but will not be troublesome. Many Asian shoppers will see it as an expression of thriftiness and, as a consequence, a visible sign that this store is inexpensive. At least 30 to 35 percent of the shoppers in a local store that looks disorderly will say that the way the products are presented gives them the feeling that the prices are cheap.

When we probe more elements that relate to cleanliness such as the restrooms, the satisfaction level goes down to 60 or 65 percent but the cause for dissatisfaction generally does not come from a lack of cleanliness per se. In fact most who complain are annoyed simply because there are not enough restroom facilities in store, or because they are difficult to find or are too small. The negative comments come from females more than from males.

Some stores offer a playground for children or a resting place. This happens in markets like Korea where shoppers are sensitive about the overall notion of service but also in less developed markets in case of large shopping malls. Those areas for children address two customer motivations: shopping and leisure. If the parents want mainly to shop they can leave the children in this environment without worrying. If the motivation is primarily entertainment, like a family outing, then the playground is part of the fun; it's an element of the mix. When there is a playground for children, about one in four shoppers will use this service, typically a mother of two, in her late thirties but she is not entirely satisfied about it (just a little over 50 percent satisfaction). Her main issue is not qualitative but quantitative. The playground is often judged too small. The secondary concern is about the safety of the playground.

Resting places for shoppers are also appreciated but in a lukewarm manner, with only 60 percent satisfaction. Here again the problem is based on a quantifiable notion. When shoppers are not satisfied, the overwhelming reason is that the resting area is too small. Very little dissatisfaction relates to the noise level or difficulty finding the resting place in the store.

## Product shortage

Last but not least among the important parameters on shopping convenience is the product availability, whether shoppers find the products they expect to buy, or whether they are out of stock.

It is not unusual to find stores in Japan or Korea where more than half of the shoppers sometimes find that their store is out of stock. One out of five of these customers even feel this happens quite often. In the rest of Asia dissatisfaction about product shortage if far less prominent, with a clear majority saying they don't experience product shortage that much, and only a very low percentage (3 or 4 percent) saying they often notice out of stock situations.

This does not necessarily mean the logistics in Korea and Japan are poorly managed, because here again, the customer response also depends on expectations. In northeast Asia, a Japanese mother considers quite strongly that the store is at her service. If she is shopping for food in order to prepare the evening meal, she will feel upset if the product she wants is *urikire* (sold out). Further south in Asia, a Thai mother in the same situation will feel more accommodating toward the store if the product she wants is not available.

This is not specifically due to cultural differences but to physical conditions. As the Japanese housewife doesn't stock much food in her small kitchen, she buys fresh products regularly. If she wants to cook tempura today, she will shop today for what she needs. She is relying on the store. Expectations also depend on the economic development of the market. In a newly industrialized country like Thailand, but also China, the Philippines, Indonesia, many of the shoppers are still used to logistics problems. In the high-low stores that offer many promotions in developing markets, the customers are also used to experiencing shortage for special offers, in particular for home cleaning products and personal care, as well as various snacks at food retailers. In non-food stores, the shortage issues are more acute in the case of ladies wear and accessories.

Customer brand loyalty explains part of the difference as well. We did not survey every single product category in every Asian country, but it seems the customers in emerging markets show less loyalty toward brands than Asian shoppers in more developed countries. Customers in Thailand, China, Indonesia, and other developing markets may want a brand that is reasonably famous, but for some shoppers, famous brands are interchangeable. If their usual product is not on the shelf, they will purchase the other well-known brand almost without noticing. We think this is one reason why shoppers in China and most of Southeast Asia complain less about product shortages. If their brand is out of stock but the product category is represented in store by other brands, shoppers don't feel there is a real shortage.

## Checkout counters

At the end of a shopping trip, shoppers pay cashiers, but the experience is also about queuing. A decade or two ago, customers in Asia had fewer problems with waiting in line than they have today. In the past, people in some Asian markets would even voluntarily spend time in a store and wait for the price rebate on some fresh produce toward the end of the afternoon, in order to buy at that time and save a little money.

Now, this is less and less true. In 2011, queuing time has not changed much, but the change is that Asian shoppers are discovering the value of their personal time and the importance of wasted minutes. Queuing in line at a hypermarket for instance, or waiting for the payment process to take place at a downtown department store have become somewhat of an inconvenience, not only in developed markets.

Overall, shoppers in Asia are still quite understanding. At large food retailers in Japan or Korea, where queues do exist and waiting time is not negligible, we still have around 65 to 70 percent satisfaction about the waiting time and the quickness of cashiers. In Southeast Asia, the satisfaction about quickness at the checkout counter ranges from 65 to 85 percent (less satisfaction in emerging markets like Vietnam, more satisfaction in developed countries like Singapore). In China, Hong Kong and Taiwan, where people are quite impatient, the satisfaction about waiting time at checkout counters is still about 70 percent.

The issue is more important for food retailers, such as supermarkets and for hypermarkets, and for department stores as well, because those outlets generate high traffic. Category killers do not attract as many visitors. If you go to a major furniture store or a large toys retailer, you will see fewer than 100 transactions per hour. A smaller specialist may generate 50 tickets per hour or less. At a hypermarket, more than 500 ticket counts per hour is not rare. However, in most cases, the satisfaction on queuing time is quite comparable for department stores, hypermarkets, and category killers. This is because a department store allocates more staff at peak time, and hypermarkets open up 30 or 40 cashier lines when necessary, while a category killer generally has half a dozen checkout counters. Hypermarkets have 5 or 6 times more customers waiting to pay at the cashiers' than specialist's stores, but also 5 or 6 times more staff members to service them.

Discontent depends on the time of the day and the day of the week. Since customers can go shopping any day including Sundays, and roughly speaking, any time between 10 a.m. and 10 p.m., the experience with checkout counter varies.

If we look at supermarkets/hypermarkets and department stores, Friday is generally bad, with a low satisfaction on waiting time at cashiers.

Both Saturday and Sunday show an average satisfaction in terms of queuing, with Saturday being just a little less satisfactory. The fact that waiting satisfaction on weekends is not worse than the rest of the week is not surprising. Combined, the two days of the weekend represent about 40 percent of the total weekly transactions and store managers allocate more cashiers than on weekdays. Yet, Saturdays are a little busier than Sundays, and even if all checkout counters are open that day, the fluidity can be less good than on Sundays.

We also notice satisfaction differences based on shopping time during the day. Quite constantly, in northeast Asia, greater China and Southeast Asia, the bad time of the day is around 7 or 8 p.m. For the same reasons as above, if there is a large number of shoppers in the store after office hours, even if the management opens more cashier lines, there is a moment when this will not be enough for satisfactory shopping, especially since everybody is particularly tired and impatient to go home.

In fact, the time spent at the checkout counter is generally an experience that is somewhat frustrating. More than two-thirds of the customers in Asia say the waiting time is acceptable or satisfactory but, when asked what the store can do in order to improve, the number one request is very often "to have more checkout counters."

## Staff competence

In Chapter 3 we followed Suzy within a hypermarket, but in parallel, her husband went to a small store that specializes in electronics and brown goods, because he wanted to check out the new 3D TV screens. Beforehand though, he had to go to the after-sales counter because he had a problem with the screen of the smartphone he bought there a few weeks before.

A young lady was in line in front of him so he had to queue a little, while a couple of other customers were behind him. The young lady needed her laptop computer fixed and while the technician was checking the device, she kept asking questions about how to set up a second email address on her mailbox, how to change the security password, and other "how-to" questions.

"You should read the how-to booklet that came with the computer," said the technician after a while.

Everybody laughed.

"I know. But it's complicated. I'm too lazy to read all this instruction manual," she replied.

When it was his turn, Suzy's husband described the issue with the screen of his phone. The light was not bright enough and it sometimes dimmed suddenly. The store technician understood and was totally willing to help. Unfortunately he had never heard of this kind of problem before and was unsure what to do.

Keep in mind this is a Sunday. The technician cannot call the manufacturer's hotline. He switches on the device while secretly hoping the screen will look normal. Then he would be able to say, "Look the brightness is OK;" it would be a quick solution. If there is no "visible" problem to solve, you cannot lose face by not solving it. It would be an easy way to say good-bye politely.

This time, the technician is not lucky; the screen is actually very dim once switched on. Seeing is believing and visibly there is some kind of real defect. The technician (also called engineer) appears to look at the smartphone, with no real clue. He knows the customer is waiting, has no answer for him, and now feels he has to find some kind of excuse. For example he will say, "Ah, it's because of the software." This again means, "Sorry there's nothing I can do," but would also mean he keeps face. If he works for the store selling electronic appliances and the problem is software, you cannot request him to do anything; the software is not his responsibility. Suzy's husband can then either say, "OK. I understand please send the smartphone to the manufacturer and keep me posted." Or he may insist and say something like, "I think software should have absolutely nothing to do with the brightness of the screen."

If so, the engineer is not likely to contradict his customer, he will look again at the screen and the whole device, touch a few things, and fiddle around. It may become a never-ending story until the client finally says, "Thank you for trying, please send it to the manufacturer."

You may think this example is a little extreme, or that Asian stores have procedures and that technicians don't waste time like this; they just write down the customer request and send the whole thing to the back office for processing next week. In fact, stores in Asia may have a step-by-step method but often, employees don't really know about it, because they are new and nobody took time to professionally train them. In many countries, the employees will work a few months in a store and then will go somewhere else, so the stores constantly employ a large ratio of new workers. Since chains are cost-conscious, they also hesitate to invest in training new staff while knowing that turnover is high. Secondly many small chains do not have such procedures at all. They focus on opening new outlets and at that stage, best practice regarding operations is not a priority. There is a third point. Local culture encourages staff to show they care, with hard work and respect for authority (the client). So if there is no practical solution at the time, the customer has to acknowledge that the staff showed respect and dedication. On his side the technician or engineer is reluctant to admit he doesn't have any solution. This is embarrassing. So the shopper has to "relieve him from duty" as it were. In our example the technician did not really fail. Nobody lost face once the client said, "Let's send it to the manufacturer." Nobody failed because the customer's pressing request disappeared, or at least became less pressing.

In general, customers in Asia are satisfied with staff competence related to the knowledge of the employee—technical knowledge as we've just seen, but also commercial knowledge and the ability to answer commercial questions (How long is the guarantee if I buy this air conditioner? Is there a free installment payment?) or simply knowledge about the store layout (Where can I find the imported gourmet foods? Where is the counter for product return?).

There is no single conclusion about satisfaction on staff competence. In some countries like Japan the ratings can appear to be very high, such as 90 percent for some departments, whereas in Korea there is less than 60 percent satisfaction with staff knowledge for the same product category, and results are in between in the other Asian markets. Customers rate staff competence based on the knowledge they display. The sales staff either knows how long the guaranty is or doesn't know; the employee knows where the exchange and refund counter is or doesn't know. The satisfaction ratings reflect this and can vary from store to store, and from store manager to store manager. However, the rating also depends on the questions asked.

In Japan, if you want to buy a washing machine, chances are that you will have the choice between five or six local brands such as Panasonic, Sharp, Toshiba, Hitachi, Sanyo, and Mitsubishi. A Japanese citizen will think the Japanese-made appliance is of good quality, and may not ask too many technical questions. As a consequence, the customer may be automatically satisfied with the salesman's knowledge. Conversely in Korea, with import liberalization in the last 15 years, customers can buy domestic washing machines but also appliances made elsewhere. About one-third of the market is imports. Korean shoppers will tend to ask questions about the quality and reliability of the foreign refrigerator or washing machine, whether it is from Europe, the U.S., or China. If the salesman is thoroughly challenged and doesn't have all the answers, he will have a low rating on product knowledge in the customer's mind. In other Asian countries too, when technical questions are asked (How does this computer work? How do you get PIP on this TV?) staff response is often disappointing.

The issue is more acute in the case of home improvement category killers, because when a customer visits, he often has a complex problem to solve. Perhaps he is not just buying a refrigerator, but a whole kitchen or bathroom or flooring. When he asks questions the customer in this case judges the DIY staff member not only on technical knowledge but also on the employee's ability to understand his specific needs. However, in the surveys we have conducted, these two attributes, "the staff are knowledgeable," "the staff understand my needs," rate approximately the same (with around 90 percent satisfaction, which is very good).

## Staff attitude

There are several parameters that help gauge the staff attitude in the eyes of customers. One is friendliness, which is clearly more emotional and subjective than competence. If the Asian culture wants harmony, one would expect the ratings on friendliness or kindness to be high. However, Asian stores are not a magical world with perfect harmony. One reason is that if Asian culture says that the customer is king, customers will expect to be treated as such. It is not always a reality though, both at upscale shopping destinations and at lower end stores. The best department store in a city will attract rich people while a discount store will capture lower income customer groups, and in both cases the challenge is to manage expectations. If the upscale department store employs staff that have been trained to be friendly and to show respect to shoppers, the friendliness ratings ratings by upper-income groups will be high, around 80 percent and sometimes up to 90 percent satisfaction on friendliness. Conversely if the staff is not trained, friendliness will show relatively weak ratings at only 60 or 55 percent, which is a huge difference from the 90 percent above.

There is a difference by countries as well. Friendliness in Asia sometimes rates very low, especially at general food retailers like hypermarkets or supermarkets—no more than 40 to 50 percent in China and Taiwan, as well as Japan, and only around 50-55 percent in Southeast Asia. It is only at department stores and upscale category killers that staff are considered quite friendly (around 75 percent at department stores) or very friendly (above 80 percent at sports, DIY and appliance specialists, including in developing markets like China). The results depend on a combination of factors including the cultural expectation in a given country, the intensity of customer flow (whether a store has a few visitors or is bustling with shoppers), and the nature of the business. It also depends, always, on the care that is taken in training the staff.

Overall, shoppers tend to rate kindness or friendliness of store employees as something that is average. In a discount store the customers may be very satisfied with prices and frustrated with the store layout but will rate the satisfaction about staff attitude somewhere in the middle. Shoppers at a category killer may be impressed by the deep assortment and dislike the product display, but they will also rate the friendliness of the employees as average. In a nutshell, the customers in Asia more or less feel that currently, stores generally don't differentiate through the employees' kindness or friendliness.

Other attitudinal measures involve staff availability and staff enthusiasm as perceived by shoppers. Store employees are often regarded as moderately enthusiastic in department stores and food retail establishments in Asia with ratings of around 65 percent, but the scores are higher at category killers (75 percent).

Whether staff members make themselves available varies more by country than by store format. Shoppers in Japan and Korea sense the store employees are generally available to serve the customers (nearly 90 percent satisfaction) but Chinese customers, both in Mainland China and Singapore rate clearly lower (70 percent) while the feeling for the other Asian customers is somewhere in between with around a 75 to 80 percent satisfaction rating on staff availability.

A last point about attitude relates to excessive commerciality, what we might call "pushiness." Retail managers in the Far East are careful not to disrupt harmony and therefore, they don't want their staff members to be too aggressive when selling. Local culture helps in the sense that employees will not want to embarrass the customers either. In Japan, for instance, they may speak loudly when promoting products in a department store, but they will not be overly annoying. In Southeast Asia, commercial aggressiveness is also relatively peaceful and is limited to store staff following customers (perhaps too closely at times). However, we must point out that in some non-food outlets (appliance stores in particular) surveys show that as much as 20 percent of the visitors feel a little too much "pressure" from the sales employees. This happens essentially in emerging economies and in rural areas of more developed markets.

We have now addressed several parameters about the commercial offer, both in terms of products and service, and reviewed how satisfactory or not satisfactory each parameter is. It is time to see among all these attributes, which ones are the most important if a store wants its customers to be loyal.

# 9

# How to Create Loyal Shoppers in Asia

FOR MANY retailers, especially when a market becomes mature, the question is, "How can I make the customers loyal?" This does not refer to loyalty cards but to customers who prefer, in their heart, to shop one store and not another. Unfortunately, there is no magic formula, but there are some findings that we can outline.

## Exclusive shoppers and membership cards don't imply loyalty

A customer may own a dozen loyalty cards, but it doesn't mean he or she is loyal to a dozen retail brands. It simply means there are benefits whenever you shop with the cards. Customers who shop almost exclusively at one store are not necessarily loyal either. They may happen to live next door and it's simply convenient to shop only at that store. There could be other reasons that are not related to the store. If the shopper does not particularly "prefer" this store for some good reason, a time will come when a competitive outlet will open in the vicinity and the store management will learn there is a difference between exclusive shopper and loyal customer.

Among other approaches, a good way to gauge the loyalty of a customer is the question that the business strategist Frederick Reichheld helped make popular: it is to ask, "Would you recommend this (store) to other people?" (*The Ultimate Question*, Harvard Business Press, 2006) Respondents have five possible answers from "yes definitely," "yes probably," "neither/nor," "no probably not," and "no definitely not."

Let's consider a customer group who shops exclusively for non-food at a certain department store. If we ask them the "would you recommend" question, and the data show about 57 to 58 percent "absolutely yes" among these exclusive shoppers with only 4 percent answering "no" it sounds pretty good. However, if in parallel we have 52 or 53 percent of the other customer group, the "non exclusive" shoppers, saying "yes, absolutely" as well (and also just 4 percent saying no), then we don't have a clear correlation between being an "exclusive shopper" and being loyal. There is a difference of a few percentage points but it's hardly a sign that shopping a store exclusively means being loyal to that outlet. In other words, both the exclusive shoppers and the non-exclusives do appreciate the store and will tend to be loyal in comparable proportions. Quite often the customers who are not exclusive shoppers are the ones who actually live further away. They have fewer opportunities to recommend the store to the neighbors, for instance.

The same can be said in the case of a supermarket. The "I would definitely recommend" ratings are roughly 50 percent in the markets we probed, whether the customers shop exclusively there or not. We have to point out that 50 percent here is lower than for a department store (around 55 percent) because a supermarket purchase is less emotional. A female shopper will be less prone to recommend a supermarket because she'll be less enthusiastic about a kilogram of tomatoes than about a fashionable dress shirt.

What happens with exclusive customers also applies to loyalty cards; roughly the same ratio of those who own a member card and those who don't will recommend a store. A customer may own and use regularly the card at a store but will not be mechanically more loyal to the retail brand than the shopper without a card. Chances are that the card member will be more loyal to the concept of accumulating points. As far as we can tell, it is the same with all store formats, not just department stores or super-markets. A category killer will achieve similar recommendation scores (around 40 percent) from card-members and non card-members as well as from exclusive and non-exclusive customers. This rating of 40 percent is lower than with other formats not so much because products bought are expensive and Asian customers are always disappointed with the price, but mostly because those are not daily necessities. At category killers that specialize in technical goods, Asian shoppers are sometimes disappointed by the lack of product knowledge among the staff. This also has an impact on the lower rating on this "would you recommend" question.

While the ratings are comparable, it doesn't mean that loyalty cards are useless. They are useful because they help the chain understand what the customers buy as the CRM example of a family buying diapers indicates. The loyalty card generates opportunities, but does not automatically induce customer preference for a chain.

Instead of "would you recommend," we can also ask customers about their satisfaction with their overall shopping experience, checking the results from the card-members and from the exclusive shoppers and comparing with the average. However, here again, the outcome is not very different. Those who are exclusive customers and those who are not, those who own a card and those who don't, will answer basically in the same way as the other customers. Having a membership card or always shopping such or such place are behavior traits; they are not particularly reliable signs of customer loyalty.

## Satisfaction does not imply loyalty either

In the previous chapters we addressed about 100 parameters that you can probe in terms of satisfaction. Those parameters need to be relatively precise. For example, the perceived value for money on fresh produce is not necessarily the same as value for money on packaged goods. The same can be said for non-food; customers in a general merchandise store may perceive the value for money differently on white goods, clothing, electronics, or the food court when there is one. Also, if we probe the price, promotions, assortment, and perceived quality on these 5 or 6 categories we measure 30 parameters or so. In each category, we also need to rate staff-member services such as their competence, friendliness, availability, quickness, or whether store employees are too laid back or overly pushy. Other variables that we can specify include the facilities such as parking lots, trolleys and baskets, ease in walking around in the store, cleanliness, presence and legibility of price labels and of store signage, lighting, air-conditioning, music, and so forth. Other possibilities are the after sales environment such as the information counter, guarantee, delivery service, exchange and refund, and communication including in-store POPs and LCD screens, direct mailings or brochures, print ads, TV commercials, and so forth. While we can measure a satisfaction level on all those parameters, it still doesn't tell much about the importance of each of these variables in terms of building loyalty. Some retailers consider that everything is important, so all the 100 variables are key, nothing is secondary. Others will say that if the store has five main issues to tackle, its managers need to concentrate on number 1 and 2, and once these are solved, to focus on 3 and 4, etc. We tend to agree with this, but the question remains, how do we know what builds customer loyalty?

Although there is no magic formula, we think there is a method, and it has to do with mathematics. When we interview shoppers, other than the 100 parameters about satisfaction, we ask questions about their shopping criteria. On what factors do they decide to buy a certain product at one place and not another place. We call this the store selection criteria. With exit surveys, we also ask shoppers about their attitude or their intentions relative to their specific store. We interview them as they just finish shopping and among the questions we ask, there are half a dozen topics focused on their loyalty toward the store. We don't ask, "Are you a loyal customer?" We ask about their overall satisfaction with the store, how they would rate the benefits of using this store compared with other outlets, and how much the store meets their expectations. We also ask how much the customers actually *like* shopping here and "Do you plan to shop here again?" and "Would you recommend this store to other people?" With the answers to these six questions, we can rate how loyal the customers are, as far as their hearts and minds are concerned.

A customer answering a strong yes to all six loyalty questions is rated as very loyal to this particular retail establishment. Conversely a customer saying strongly no to all of these will be considered as not being loyal. We then cross-reference the loyal and the non-loyal ratings with the satisfaction scores. For instance, we may notice that customers who are non-loyal tend to rate the store employees as unfriendly or not courteous, while the loyal customers feel that the employees are very friendly. If the statistical correlation is high, then we have a hint that in this specific outlet, a friendly experience with the store staff will generate loyalty.

This method is interesting because it is focused on attitudes and goes beyond behaviors, which as we saw with card-members and exclusive shoppers, can be misleading. The method has a limitation though. Even if you first ask about store selection factors and then cross reference the satisfaction levels with five or six loyalty questions, you can always interpret that there is no correlation. For instance, if the above example seems to show that a friendly experience with employees builds customer loyalty, you may claim that there is no real corroboration; loyal shoppers happen to say they like the store employees, non-loyal shoppers happen to say they don't, and that's just coincidence.

However, the correlations we observe for same format stores are comparable in different countries. We think there is a correspondence between the ratings that show loyalty in terms of attitude and actual customer loyalty as a behavior. For each type of store format in food and non-food, we have completed a set of correlations that indicate the customer satisfaction levels for each element probed (staff friendliness for instance) and the impact of the element on building loyalty. We can then display the parameters in four different groups:

- Parameters that show high satisfaction and high loyalty building

- Parameters that show low satisfaction, but high loyalty building

- Parameters that show high satisfaction but low loyalty building

- Parameters that show a low satisfaction and low impact on loyalty building

In return, the findings can help recommend what the retail establishments should aim for when they want to improve customer loyalty. This methodology does not provide specific percentages; for example one cannot conclude that parameter A builds 22 percent loyalty or 63 percent loyalty but it contributes nevertheless rather clearly. It says whether parameter A appears to be a relatively strong loyalty builder or whether it is quite inconsequential. The process can be applied to various store concepts and formats and help determine what the challenges are for each type of store for customer retention.

## Supermarkets: Try to differentiate with imported foods

A supermarket is usually rather small, with a net sales area of about 1,000–2,000 square meters. Because of this, its catchment area is not large, and most of its sales actually come from customers who live within 6 or 8 minutes distance, not 15 or 20 minutes. Quite a few supermarkets are located in shopping malls and as such they benefit from the large catchments of the malls but even in those cases where their catchment area corresponds to 20 minutes, most of their business comes from shoppers who live in proximity. On average, Asian customers who live 6 or 8 minutes away will shop their supermarkets about twice a week, whereas the same customer goes to a shopping mall only two to three times a month. At the end of the year, what makes a difference for the supermarket is the customers who shop with a high frequency and those are the people who live close by.

So whenever we look at a supermarket we have to consider the proximity zones and whether the neighborhood is relatively wealthy or relatively poor. In wealthy areas, supermarket customers consider that store signage and staff competence, for instance, are important for them to remain loyal. In less wealthy areas customers focus more on staff friendliness than store signs. In terms of merchandise, both the richer and poorer pay attention to fresh products; the freshness and perceived quality, especially for fish, fruits, and vegetables is vital to build customer loyalty. Higher income customers tend to show a little more loyalty when the supermarket offers a selection of high quality wines and spirits, whereas for the less wealthy shoppers this has little effect on loyalty building.

However, in both rich and poor neighborhoods, money is an issue and impacts customer loyalty. Price and promotions are always among the parameters with high "loyalty-building" power, as is assortment. In all catchment areas, the customer response at supermarkets show that product variety is one of the main parameters that help build loyalty, both in affluent and less affluent zones. Not only do Asian customers appreciate a large selection of fresh and packaged foods, but they also love the modern and new items. This is an opportunity for supermarkets in countries where people have a high living standard or growing purchasing power because it is an avenue for imported goods. Shoppers in Asia have a perception that imported foods from Western countries and from Japan (in the case of customers who reside in Greater China and Southeast Asia) have a good quality and this is confirmed with satisfaction ratings during surveys. A large selection of imported wines will not have much impact on loyalty building for most supermarkets though because wine does not attract everyone in Asia. In upscale supermarkets, shoppers may appreciate the presence of a selection of wine and spirits (and may show more loyalty to that supermarket as a side effect), but they are not necessarily wine lovers so the actual sales of wine and spirits will not always be important.

The categories of imported products that have good potential for loyalty-building and for sales are the ones that are considered not only high quality but also affordable. For example, they include all kinds of imported sweets (candies, chocolate, various confections), frozen foods (ice cream but also frozen meals, frozen vegetables, seafood, etc.), imported dairy, processed meats, and organic foods, as well as imported sashimi, which does not always need to come from Japan but can be imported from China, Taiwan, Korea, and as far south as Indonesia.

## Hypermarkets: Make shopping easier and diversify the non-food selection

Large supercenters or hypermarkets with about 6,000 to 10,000 square meters of net sales area do not depend on the neighborhood as much as supermarkets do. They can achieve more sales from people who live beyond the primary zone than from the residents in proximity. The first reason is that a large store that offers all you need under one roof can attract customers who reside relatively far away, even beyond 20 minutes driving distance. Typically 80 percent of the customers will prefer one-stop-shopping instead of going to multiple stores (and this is even more so among customers with higher income and higher educational levels than average). The second reason is that in Asia, most shoppers go to hypermarkets to buy necessities and on average they go there once every two weeks, not once a week. No matter whether customers live nearby or far away, and whether or not they are wealthy, their basket is not too different. With this in mind, a hypermarket needs to be easily accessible. Whether it is established in a rich part of town versus a poorer zone doesn't matter as much as for supermarkets.

What comes to light with the loyalty-building analysis is that in both emerging and developed countries, and for stores in both large cities and smaller towns up-country, the customer response in Asia shows a relatively constant pattern for what builds loyalty at a hypermarket.

First, human interactions are important. Friendliness, competence, and availability of sales staff are almost always among the top elements that have an impact on loyalty. In countries where people tend to be impatient like the Chinese markets, ease of finding staff will actually be more important and in other markets, the data show that staff friendliness and knowledge will make shoppers more loyal. Again, this does not mean the customers feel the store employees are wonderful. Far from it. It simply shows that employee attitude in the Far East can be a major part of the shopping experience at hypermarkets, especially when the staff facilitate shopping.

The other common trait across Asian markets is a shopping visit that is easy and practical. Ease of finding products and store signage, for instance, are almost always key points at hypermarkets because they help save time for a customer. Speed at checkout is another of the elements that will make shoppers more or less loyal. The only cases when checkout speed has virtually no impact is for medium-size supercenters that serve a local community often with a population that is older than average. In those cases, people shop there as a matter of habit, there is virtually no out-of-zone customer, and life is not hectic. But other than that, the speed at checkout counters is an important part of the need for practicality at hypermarkets.

What matters less in this store format relates to comfort. Whether the trolleys roll perfectly is not crucial. The same can be said for the parking facility, the restrooms, the general shopping environment, store cleanliness, the width of aisles or the cartons sometimes scattered in the customer's path. All those elements can be annoying if they are not managed perfectly, but an Asian customer will not decide to stop visiting an outlet because it's hard to walk around in the store. Asian customers want to save time, they want to deal with human beings in the store, but they can accept some lack of comfort at the hypermarket.

All this is true also for the warehouse concept stores like Costco. The only difference is that there is a membership card that is compulsory. You have to pay a fee at the beginning of the year and Asian shoppers are a bit ambivalent about this must-have card. The negative point as mentioned earlier is they feel it is expensive even though it can be refunded if they are not happy. The positive point is the merchandise offered. A warehouse concept offers fewer SKUs than a hypermarket but will sell lots of unique items, because of the private labels, the imported goods, or because some items are more up-to-date and trendy than elsewhere. This is the justification for paying the membership fee.

For hypermarkets and warehouse concepts, the prices and the assortment play a role in loyalty building but are not always satisfactory. The issue of assortment is relatively simple. Shoppers at hypermarkets want a deep choice of both food and non-food. In particular they want to see a variety of national and international brands as opposed to just store brands or private labels, which may represent 10 percent of sales at hypermarkets but they do not build customer loyalty. At hypermarkets, quality is not among the main loyalty-building elements. For non-food and packaged foods like groceries, this is understandable because customers think a specific brand offers the same quality in all outlets. With fresh produce, quality is also not a determinant to building loyalty at hypermarkets. This may sound counter intuitive, but Asian customers often feel that fresh is not a *forte* of hypermarkets and that those stores are great for grocery but it's better to buy fresh foods elsewhere. Let's keep in mind that unlike European hypermarkets where almost one third of sales are related to fresh, the ratio in Asia is three times less. Asian shoppers expect fresh to be just okay at hypermarkets, but not exceptional, which is why fresh does not build much loyalty.

If we look at more detail, clothing is the product category for which a large choice can build loyalty at a hypermarket. Asian customers have a perception that all supercenters provide a large selection of packaged goods and that they don't fully differentiate on groceries or personal care items. If a generalist can offer a wide selection of clothing, there is a chance to capture and retain customers more strongly than the competition.

In general, price is also a loyalty-building element at hypermarkets and discount stores and this applies to virtually all products. Asian customers pay attention to how much food costs, because those are daily necessities. On the other hand, females especially pay attention to apparel prices. They like to see, check, and see again, dream, compare prices, check again, on clothing in as many stores as possible before purchasing. The price of appliances as well is loyalty building, because even though home equipment is not bought frequently, they are expensive and require some rational thought process. The only category for which price is not loyalty building at hypermarkets is hard goods because you don't buy a broom every day and the cost is not very high.

## Department stores: Surprise your customers

Not unlike hypermarkets, department stores are generalists that sell almost everything under one roof, but they are not discount stores. This concept, more than a century old, is to display a wide but also deep assortment with multiple items (around 150,000 SKUs) at fixed prices. If you want apparel, for instance, you can find a basic shirt at a hypermarket, but you can choose from dozens of dress shirts at a department store, with various styles and features, at different price points that are fixed.

The customer segments at department stores are different from those at hypermarkets in terms of income. They earn about 20 to 25 percent more on average and they shop not only in order to buy necessities but also as a leisure activity. There is an element of joy when actually making a purchase. At a department store, Asians feel it is fun to seek products and to find something you like, or to buy on impulse. About 60 percent come with a plan to look around in the store, but not knowing if they will buy something or even what brands or products they might want. Therefore, at a department store the shopping environment plays an important role and is always among the top elements that build customer loyalty. The more upscale the department store is, the more important the environment.

Together with the overall shopping atmosphere and fixtures, the variety of products and brands will also determine customer loyalty. In developing countries where counterfeits are rampant, a department store provides reassurance that the merchandise is genuine. In the rest of the shopping mall, a shopper can find pirated products but not in the department store itself. In markets that are more mature, shoppers look for premium brands. In both developing and emerging markets, product quality is key and both width and depth of the range will be major loyalty-building parameters.

There are two requirements in that respect. Asian customers want to see products that offer something new and are well displayed.

New does not necessarily mean fashionable; it's about impulse; it is what a customer (80 percent female) will feel is up to date, even if it is not in line with international fashion. Well displayed is partly rational (to make it easy to find products), but is mostly emotional since more than half of the customers don't know in advance what they want to buy. Unlike for discount stores or traditional markets, customers don't want to see bulk display tables or vending carts in a department store. For them, well displayed means eye-catching merchandise, something that will be pleasant to see. They want to be surprised, but not by checking through lots of undifferentiated piles of products on shelf.

Staff members too play a part in building customer loyalty for department stores, but not in terms of saving time. Staff availability, quickness of cashiers, staff enthusiasm will not make shoppers more loyal. What will count is the competence of staff members and their friendliness; both elements are equally important. Usually it is relatively easy to train employees to be polite and hospitable and it is easy to have knowledgeable staff, but both points build, or damage, customer loyalty in the case of a department store. Another (secondary) element about staff in these retail establishments is whether they are too pushy. In Asia a store employee will not be overly aggressive as we said, except in small cities in emerging markets where about 20 percent of the customers feel they are "followed too closely." However, in department stores in the Far East, if customers feel the employees are a bit too aggressive or follow them, it is annoying but it is fair to say that it does not have a significant effect on refusing to visit the outlet again.

## Perfume, cosmetic and soft-line retailers: Provide creative content

Retail establishments that specialize in selling perfumes and those that sell shoes or garments or personal care have comparable customer segments with department stores, in terms of income and age groups, except that they are even more segmented. The loyalty-building parameters are also similar in terms of employees and merchandise. As in a department store, the customers expect staff to be friendly and knowledgeable. For instance, an employee has to be able to do a product demonstration and to talk about the fragrances or to know what is the strong point of a particular fabric in the case of apparel. Excessive pushiness does not affect loyalty very much. If anything, the customers feel it means the employees are there to answer questions and they associate this behavior with staff-member availability.

In these smaller outlets, shoppers don't make a pre-planned purchase, and more than half will buy spontaneously, about the same proportion as for department stores. The top element that will trigger impulse purchase is the variety of styles.

The layout and the overall environment of the small outlets (from around 100 to a few hundred square meters) is also important to create shopper loyalty. Customers visiting an apparel shop or a perfume special-ist don't focus on the rational aspects of the visit such as ease in finding products, store lighting, or product labels. In these relatively small outlets, customers don't feel they might waste time. Besides, if they visit a specific boutique, they are interested in virtually all the items displayed, which does not mean they plan to buy but at least they want to extensively review the offering. So even if it is a little bit uneasy to locate products or if the price tags are not very legible, shoppers in small stores will not mind too much. Here, most of the shopping experience is emotional, not rational, and the practical side of the shopping environment will not be as crucial as with department stores. On the other hand the presence of new products is vital and expected.

What is key for small stores specializing in emotional offers relates primarily to a quick turnaround of the products. Shoppers here want a display that is pleasant, more than just functional, and they also want pleasant and knowledgeable staff members. Beyond that, the customers want to see novelties, a deep assortment with something trendy and modern each time they visit. For instance, up-to-date garments with various styles, or a selection of different sizes of vials and bottles at a perfume store will encourage shoppers to come again and to become loyal customers. Customers go to these outlets less than once per month, so when they do visit, specialized stores need to show some kind of new arrivals, by constantly adapting and modifying the offer with high quality items that are affordable.

One way to do this in Asia is to develop lines of licensed products endorsed by a celebrity. We have not encountered many customers in Asia who would reject a product endorsed by a celebrity who is liked. Even customers that don't particularly appreciate an actor, actress, or singer, will not reject a co-branding between a product and the celebrity's name. The need is not to find a superstar; it is to find an artist who is socially accepted and who has a specific image that can be leveraged. In each Far East country there are dozens of local celebrities who are popular. Asian celebrities usually behave in appropriate ways and rarely trigger scandals; the low risk level is another reason to consider co-branding or licensing. For many specialized retail brands, the opportunity exists and what they need to do is to find a match between a local star, what he or she stands for, and the customer segments and then to position the celebrity-endorsed product accordingly. It should be affordable with high quality. The point with local singers or actors endorsing a product is also that the artists provide cultural content that is constantly refreshed so the retailer does not need to develop internal creative content and indirectly benefits from constant exposure. While retail chains don't usually develop co-branding by themselves, (producers do), retailers can still differentiate their products by having specific contracts with the brand owners to use celebrities.

## Category killers: Showcase your expertise

There are many kinds of category killers since virtually any product family can be regrouped in some way in a store. For example a retail brand can specialize in all types of cultural products and sell books, CDs, and DVDs as well as electronics and brown goods under the same roof. It is reasonable to consider that a TV set, a video game console, a portable computer, a GPS, or a smartphone are all tools that help communicate with others and, in this regard, are actually cultural products. Such a brand can sell museum tickets and seats to all types of shows as well, since those are cultural products too. Yet a theater ticket and a laptop computer have very little in common as a product category.

Now let's focus on category killers that relate to home interior or to durable goods, such as furniture retailers, DIY and home improvement specialists, and appliance stores.

Price and promotions are not always loyalty-building parameters in those cases. The promotions should not be considered negligible, but they do not trigger customer loyalty because the products are bought for a purpose that is rational. Price and promotion play a less dominant role at those outlets in terms of customer loyalty than at the other formats.

Practicality is another variable that is nice but not really critical at those stores. If it is not easy to find the products, if the shopping carts are not perfect, or if the product labeling is a bit unclear, a shopper will be annoyed but will not decide to stop visiting because of this.

Conversely the human factor is loyalty building. At a furniture store the customers don't expect a bed or a table to be highly technical and they don't feel the need to ask many technical questions. But they want to see friendly staff. It is also the case at home improvement stores. Shoppers, especially males, know a few things about DIY or feel they do, so they mostly expect the store employees to be kind and available. But if the employees are not very knowledgeable it is acceptable. The aspect of behavior of store employees that almost always builds loyalty at category killers is friendliness and enthusiasm. Ideally, in the case of a chain that is a specialist, the staff members should be more than just friendly; they should be passionate about their products.

The other elements that build customer loyalty at category killers could be called brand expertise or professionalism. If a store sells white goods and brown goods, the product quality is not a key issue. As we have seen, if customers in a country consider that Sony is a great brand or LG is a great brand, then the store simply has to make those brands available. In that case the retail brand needs to appear as professional as possible both in store and out of the store. In store, a shopping environment that is clean and user-friendly is needed, with enthusiastic and polite employees, ideally some of them having a good technical knowledge as well. Out of the store, professionalism is needed in advertisements and at the call center, which is a significant point of contact with customers. To a lesser extent, the delivery and installation process also needs to be executed with care.

If the retailer is a DIY specialist, expertise involves two things: quality of the products and quality of the solution offered. A store selling paint, power tools, bathroom equipment, or plumbing material does not always benefit from brands that are well known and trusted. There are lots of brands for bathtubs, ceramic tiles, doors, windows, and all other types of DIY products but Asian customers won't necessarily know which ones are reputable. On the other hand, if they feel they can rely upon the chain to stock high-quality products and provide good advice, the category killer will have loyal customers. The quality of the solution offered involves customers who need more than DIY and require added value service from specialized employees, not the employees who refill the shelves. For instance, when a customer wants to remodel the whole kitchen, the need will involve flooring, kitchen cabinets, some appliances, as well as design advice; it goes far beyond the purchase of a few buckets of paint.

In many Asian countries, as we saw in Chapter 1, when people buy an apartment, they actually acquire an empty shell; almost everything still needs to be done in the new home. At that time, through its in-house designers, the home improvement store will compete with independent contractors and designers, and will aim to offer a complete solution to the new homeowner, from initial design of the various cabinets and equipment, to delivery and installation, to after-sales service. Expertise in this case means the store has to provide not only a range of high-quality products but also a variety of drawings and models with the looks and styles appreciated locally. The designer service from the store will be crucial to build customer loyalty because a few years after purchase, just three or four years in many cases, the homeowner will typically need to renovate something.

There is a form of life cycle. In a country like China (at least in large cities), but also in countries and markets that are more mature, the residents who buy a home will do some renovation every four to eight years. Such renovations are not minor projects. They may involve remodeling the kitchen, or rewiring, or some new furniture, and the budget may correspond to roughly one month of the household's income. If at the time of such renovation, the customer remembers he had a good experience with the store's design center a few years before, he will come to the same DIY store again. Therefore the category killer has to provide both the products and the service and needs to ensure the shoppers know about this. As many as 25 percent of the customers in Asia don't know about the designer service at a good home improvement chain even though there is one. Conversely when customers do know about such design center, this service is one of the top three loyalty-building elements for the DIY store.

Delivery and installation on the other hand don't really build loyalty for category killers. Whether it is an appliance specialist, a home improvement retailer, or a furniture store, customers are generally quite dissatisfied with the delivery or with the installation, but they sometimes consider these services are outsourced and they don't attribute this experience to the store, it doesn't damage the loyalty toward the retailer. Nevertheless, category killers could develop their own delivery and installation logistics and thus differentiate. The sub-categories that would be most appreciated by customers in this case are doors, windows and air-conditioning equipment: these currently show the lowest satisfaction levels especially at the stage of installation.

## Leisure products: Focus on modernity

Under the term leisure, we group stores selling sporting goods, toys, games, and editorial products such as books, magazines, CDs, and DVDs.

Those stores often face the challenge of a small sales area (a few to several hundred square meters) but also the need to offer a significant number of items (4,000 to 10,000 SKUs). The convenience of shopping is important if the stores want to have loyal customers.

Indeed those are the only outlets that we have probed in Asia where the practical aspect of shopping builds loyalty. Customers at good stores of leisure and editorial products usually say it's quite easy to find products. It is not only the general shopping environment or the ambiance that counts, but the sheer process of finding the items the customers want.

Ease in finding products appears more important than promotions or prices at those stores in terms of building loyalty and appears to be as important as the staff-member friendliness and knowledge.

However, quick staff response does not seem to be a notable factor. When Asian customers visit a specialist outlet like a toy retailer or a bookstore, they go there for a reason. It can be browsing (the same can be said about the category killers selling home improvement or furniture) or it can be for a specific purchase. In both cases the customers don't go there to save time, so if it takes a little bit of time for staff to understand and address the needs or if the checkout counter is slow, it will not matter. What does matter is staff competence and staff friendliness, roughly at par.

As to merchandise, customers don't necessarily demand a major variety of products, not even a deep variety of brands, even for toy stores. Of course shoppers want a reasonable selection but they also recognize that these outlets are relatively small, so they don't physically expect more SKUs. Also, customers don't come frequently to these establishments. A customer, not a browser, at a toy store will come less than once per month and for bookstores or sporting goods outlets it's approximately the same. The exception is those located in a downtown department store or shopping mall, which is an attractive destination, in which case they benefit from the visit frequency of the flagship store.

Customers don't ask for an overly huge assortment at leisure outlets, but each time they go, they expect that some products will be different from their last visit. They want to find the most recent novel by their favorite author or the new sport shoes that are advertised on TV or the latest action figure on the market, as long as it is affordable. Modernity or "up-to-dateness" as it were, is the other loyalty building parameter in addition to finding products and a human touch.

Elements like exchange and refund, membership card, or information about other things than the actual products, like details about the promotions or the guarantee, are quite secondary.

A last element to underscore is the educational value. Whenever possible, a leisure store will improve it's chances to create loyal customers with an array of either "edutainment" products, for toy stores; training or explanation about improving the customers' sporting ability (video LCDs showing how to perform a good swing with a golf club for instance); or, for a bookstore a large display of self-improvement books regarding topics that are aspirational (computer skills, learning English, and business or marketing management).

If there are one hundred points of contact or more between a store and its shoppers, the retailer should not conclude that there are 100 parameters and all are equivalent. In some outlets a pleasant ambiance will be important and will build loyalty; in others, comfort matters less than sheer convenience of shopping. In some stores, the customers need sales staff to be experts, in others a visitor mainly expects employees to greet them and be affable, to show that they care even when they don't have an answer. Depending on store concepts and formats, operations need different priorities if they want to secure loyal customers, but for all store formats there is a common theme: retailers need to facilitate life for the shoppers. This can be achieved either by helping customers save time or helping the visitors find the goods that are relevant to them. Asian shoppers want to see merchandise that will capture their imagination or at least activate an interest, within a friendly, agreeable environment. If seeing is believing, then it makes sense that for each store format, the customers want to see products and to be surrounded by products. And in a world where harmony is a strong value, it also makes sense that shoppers want to deal with friendly and hospitable staff.

Going forward, will these cultural traits remain? In the next one or two generations, can stores build customer loyalty with the same priorities as the ones we addressed in this chapter? Let's review these questions.

# 10

# A Few Words about the Future

IN THEORY it should be relatively easy for a store to be successful in the Far East. Customers in the region are either affluent or live in markets where the economy is growing. People are generally open to modern concepts and are looking for merchandise to buy, including new products. The trends are particularly good for modern trade because in the case of food, the diet of Asian customers is evolving toward packaged goods (breakfast cereals and dairy products, for instance, are now common) and toward international brands in the case of non-food.

One of the key elements to keep in mind for retail is that whatever the store format, customers will have just three decisions to make: shop here or not, and if yes, how frequently, and with what level of expenditure. A theoretical formula captures this behavior.

## The PR x SF x AT formula

In Chapter 4, we discussed what makes a good location for a store and these three key challenges once a store is open:

- Penetration Rate (PR),
- Shopping Frequency (SF), and
- Average Ticket (AT).

At retail a good location will essentially help the penetration rate. If the outlet is not too far from dense population centers, easy to access, and so forth, this will help the retailer capture a fair number of residents. So before even opening a store, the "penetration rate battle" can be already won or lost depending on the care and attention paid to selecting a site for a shopping mall or a stand-alone store. Selecting a good location is not sufficient though, and a retailer also has to offer a product mix that meets local demand in terms of assortment and pricing as well as service attributes that make the shopping experience pleasant. The retailer will need for example to train employees on at least one dimension: to be nice and amicable toward customers or to be experts and passionate about what they sell. Those are, we think the main issues that determine penetration rate and all this can be gauged through research.

The second variable, frequency of shopping, can be considered either in terms of number of shopping visits in a year or as an actual frequency measured by weeks for instance, but in any case it refers to how many transactions are achieved within a certain time period. Here, too, the location of a store can help. If it can be accessed by subway or other public transport the customers may visit more often than if it isn't. However, other attributes have a positive effect on frequency of shopping, such as the freshness in the case of food items. For both food and non-food, the depth of assortment can increase shopping frequencies too because, for the same basic need a customer can visit often and always find a slightly different item. We have seen that promotions, and the frequency of promotions in particular, can also have an effect on the number of shopping visits because in Asia customers are looking for something new.

If a store has a certain ratio of customers who are Bargain Lovers, for instance, and they tend to visit the store every ten days, the retailer might want to change promotions based on that frequency. If the retailer sells expensive items, the promotional rotation could be every fifteen days, because the shoppers who visit every ten days don't want to spend too much on one visit. They can instead come and buy twice within the fifteen-day promotional period. If the products sold are relatively inexpensive the promotions could be changed every week. Indeed, if Bargain Lovers see a two-for-one offer on plastic bowls they may well buy four units right away, but it might not be the case with four electrical fans, even if two are sold at the price of one. The non-verbal message toward the customers does not need to be, "We think of you every day" (especially if customers don't visit on a daily basis) but it can be, "You'll be surprised and delighted every week."

The last variable—average ticket—is difficult to tackle. Once a store is open, in a matter of weeks, less than two months usually, the catchment area is established. This means that if a department store or a hypermarket is going to have 30 percent penetration, it has reached that level in its second month of activity. It also means that if during the first few weeks of operation, shoppers start spending a certain amount, their average ticket will not change easily (except due to inflation). For daily necessities and personal needs, customers basically know what product categories they want to buy and they purchase about the same amount on each shopping visit. In the case of food retail, department stores, many category killers such as retailers for toys, apparel, sportswear or sporting goods, and bookstores the average ticket does not change much over time. This is because Asian customers have an unwritten budget in their minds for personal needs. If they are used to spending the equivalent of USD 30 per shopping visit, they may spend USD 36–38 once in a while, but will be reluctant to spend USD 50 or 60 on one visit. The average ticket is an amount that is quantifiable, whereas a shopping frequency is not so easily quantified. Asian stores selling products for personal needs can aim for a higher number of visits more easily than aiming for a higher ticket.

For big-box category killers that address home needs it is different. A household may buy a TV set at the end of the year, then a coffee machine and a rice cooker six months later, and then nothing at any appliance store for the following two years. We think that the way to increase the average ticket within a same store and a same sales area is to introduce new products from time to time and to make sure those are high-quality items, as long as the quality can be measured by Asian shoppers. This refers to the low-end paper cup in Chapter 7, for instance. If the store sells a new disposable paper cup that is cheap but it leaks and the user has to consume two cups for one use, there will be no repeat sales. But if the cup doesn't leak (i.e., a tangible benefit that the customer can measure) then the shopper will buy again and again and the store will generate additional sales. In other words, the store cannot cheat the Asian customer when the quality is something palpable that he or she can actually quantify.

PR x SF x AT = **Sales** is a formula that retailers in the Far East need to keep in mind because it helps them to think about how they can leverage each variable—penetration, frequency, ticket. Chains can experiment with several types of initiatives and benefits to see which ones have an impact on the average ticket, or on frequency of shopping or on the penetration rate. Technically retailers can measure this either through customer exit surveys or by studying the behavior based on the data from the card membership when they operate one.

## The notion of quantity

We have seen that for Asians in general and for Asian customers in particular, people are likely to be first-degree and will often judge based on quantity, on things they feel they can measure. In that respect, sight is a major sense, more than hearing or the sense of smell.

Customers in Asia can see the price of the products at modern trade and obviously pay attention to the amount of money they have to pay, but it would be too simple to conclude that in the Far East price is the only thing that matters. A statement such as "in Asia, value for money is critical" would be more accurate in our view and would accord more with the behaviors we observe. However, the key point here is that "value" for Asians does not pertain so much to quality as it does to quantity. When seeing is believing, bigger is better. Of course, this has to be in context. For a family residing in a 60 square meter apartment like an average household in large cities in Japan, what is better for the (small) refrigerator is a 25 cl. can of soda, not a two liter bottle.

The notion of quantity also explains why, in the case of fresh produce, customers in the Far East may differentiate between *quality* and the actual *freshness.* When we discuss this with them, Asian retailers are often proud that, in their country, their customers are so sophisticated. Not only are the customers quality-conscious but also they are freshness-conscious. In fact they are freshness-conscious because freshness can be quantified. You can indicate on a label the time of delivery, or the time when the cabbage or the lettuce was harvested, or when the bread was baked. It is clear and easy to see, whereas deciding that the product tastes delicious is much more uncertain. And customers in Asia do not like uncertainty.

Another aspect about quantity is what we may call the distribution network. In any given country in Asia, or in a territory like a region or a province, if a chain is clearly the leader, customers will tend to rationalize why this particular retailer is number one. People will explain that the chain is much better at addressing such or a particular need or local taste. They may be right if the number two chain is really offering a bad service of some sort, but often there is no strong evidence about a much better or much worse assortment or pricing or any other element of the marketing mix. Very often the leader is simply doing a reasonably good job and so is the number two. In those cases, the difference is that the leader entered the market first and secured the best sites for its stores. Or, the difference is based on economies of scale. If it is cheaper to open stores with Chain A than Chain B, Company A will have a chance to grow faster, especially in emerging markets.

This is somewhat important when we interview potential customers and try to know what chains or restaurants they would like in a new shopping mall. In many cities of China, as well as new and emerging markets like Cambodia, a typical customer has a better chance of seeing quick service restaurants selling fried chicken than one selling hamburgers, one reason being that a chicken franchise is cheaper to open and to operate. When we interview residents and ask which fast food outlets they would like at the new mall, if 70 percent answer they'd wish to have a KFC and only 25 percent would like a McDonald's, you cannot automatically conclude that KFC has a much greater potential.

Some people locally will try to explain that for some cultural reasons the Chinese, or the Cambodian residents in Phnom Penh, have a clear preference for fried chicken over hamburgers or that a restaurant with red color codes will be more attractive than something that looks like golden arches, but in fact, you have to be careful with interpretation. One point is true: Except for Koreans, Asians eat much more poultry than beef. For 2011, the U.S. Department of Agriculture estimates per capita beef and veal consumption at 37 Kg in the United States and 17 Kg in the EU-27. However, in countries like China, the Philippines or Taiwan veal and beef consumption is only 5 or 6 Kg per capita. It is around 10 Kg in Japan, nearly 15 Kg in Korea, and nearly 25Kg in Hong Kong. For poultry (broiler meat) the numbers show 44Kg in the United States, 18Kg for the EU-27, about 10Kg in China and the Philippines, whereas Japan and Korea are at 16 Kg, and even more in Taiwan (27 Kg) and Hong Kong (47 Kg). As a consequence, all else being equal, a quick service restaurant with a menu based on chicken that can be consumed with rice has tradition-ally more chance of attracting customers than one offering beef that is eaten with a bun.

Another point is also true: In Asian markets beef is becoming more popular and its consumption is growing rapidly, including hamburgers. In 2000, Far East residents consumed about 37.7 Kg of meat per capita in total (including poultry, beef and other meats), the projection for 2030 is 58.5 Kg according to the Food and Agriculture Organization of the United Nations. Some Far East countries are among the fastest growing markets for hamburger restaurants. So we have to interpret with caution, region by region, whenever we have a 70 percent versus 25 percent in surveys in favor of QSR offering fried chicken. It can denote a habit in taste, but it can also reflect the current predominance and exposure of one fast food brand over the other at the time of interview. It's not automatically about a preference on taste or about a better customer experience. Customers are also saying, in some cases, that they are quantity-oriented. If there are more fried chicken restaurants right now in the area, then the respondents to a survey will opt for fried chicken QSR.

One element of interpretation remains valid, though. If more than two-thirds of the residents express a wish to have some kind of international quick service restaurant, it reflects the desire for them to be "worldly," to be open to a modern shopping experience in a building that is air conditioned and organized, that displays fixed prices and that offers products from around the world. In an interview in Vientiane, Laos, a resident summed up this feeling and aspiration with a simple sentence:

> *"I think civilization means increasing the number of shopping centers in Vientiane, so that people don't go to neighboring countries to shop."*

## A problem with trust

Nearly 2,500 years ago, a little after the time of Confucius and 8,000 kilometers away, Plato made a distinction between what he called the intelligible world and the visible world. The intelligible world was that of concept and of precision while the visible world, consisting of what we see, was uncertain and always changing.

At some level, this paved the way to Western civilization because concepts lead to exact sciences and to the rule of law. Regarding commerce, it led to the notion of contracts that aim to fix and make immutable the business interactions between partners. Conversely, one could say the visible world prevailed in the Far East. Exact sciences did not thrive until Asians had contact with Westerners, and, historically, for many citizens in Asia, the rule of law was no more than the rule of the prince. Xu Jing, a Chinese minister who lived in the second century A.D., believed for example that the key principle was to "urge the people to obey the government and live quietly and at ease." As for contracts, until the twentieth century, the sheer concept of firm commitment was not welcome in Asia because it underscores uncertainty. In a world where everything is uncertain and changing, how can we commit to anything in a written and signed document?

In 2011 however, there are laws and there are contracts in Asia. And if you consider technology an exact science, the Far East hosts some of

184 Shopping Behavior in Asia

the best high-tech companies in the world. So it would seem everything has changed.

Except that, for many Asian customers, in the back of their mind at least, uncertainty still prevails when it comes to human interactions. Most Westerners already know that for Chinese businessmen, what matters is personal relations, called *guanxi*. In the rest of Asia too, everybody likes to use the phrase, "What counts is not what you know, it's who you know." A personal network is useful everywhere obviously. However, in Asia we could say that it underscores the cultural notion that it is difficult to trust someone and the ones you can trust are the people you already know (and even then, there are exceptions). It is not that people like being tricky. The vast majority of Asians are decent and generous people, but if you think about the cultural guidelines that say you must work hard, respect authority, and preserve harmony it implies that there is a price to pay. When the culture says you cannot rock the boat, you tend not to address or solve a personal problem. In the long run you may actually jeopardize genuine harmony. The other consequence is that you never know if the respect that is shown is sincere, if the visible harmony is real, and if what you are told is true.

In many Japanese novels, there are dialogues in which the characters express various opinions and afterwards, each protagonist is depicted wondering what the other character's opinion was in reality (*He said this but what did he mean really?*) The protagonists don't take what they are told as face value. There is a phrase for this: *Honne Tatemae*, which means, more or less, "what is originally true, within you" versus "what you show, or façade." It is the same in most social situations, not only in Japan. Asian people tend not to scrutinize others, but to observe each other to gauge what is their real point of view or intention. The culture compels individuals to avoid embarrassment and expressing potential conflict, and to ensure everybody keeps face. It is difficult to know if any attitude reflects a genuine opinion.

Someone in a position of authority such as a client or a boss may abuse this cultural politeness, and take advantage of it. For instance, clients may decide not to pay 100 percent of what they owe. Even if the work was well done, the supplier may then have to settle for the 70 percent received as down payment. The client feels he got a discount and the supplier, if he can survive despite losing 30 percent, may decide not to sue the client, so as to maintain visible harmony and not to show disrespect. It is also possible that both will find an arrangement and the client pays only say, 15 percent, although a court judgment would make him pay the whole amount plus interest. As Austin Coates put it, "the traditional 'notion of justice' doesn't pursue hard judgments (good for one party bad for the other) but aims for compromises that may be unsatisfactory but with a likelihood of harmonious results." (*Myself a Mandarin*, Heinemann Educational Books, 1978.)

In our example above, if the supplier does business with this client again, he might then quote a price of 120 (instead of 100, which would be the fair price) and explain this with a white lie of some sort. While they may continue doing business together, neither will trust the other.

At retail in the Far East, we think the suspicion is the same and that Asian customers do not necessarily trust either the brands or the chains. In the region, *famous* brand does not mean *trusted* brand. In China, customers may prefer to buy a Chinese brand of milk but this will be mostly for patriotic reasons, not because of trust. And if there is a scandal about contaminated milk, as in 2008–2009, the trust level will not become any better. At the time of the nuclear plant accident in Fukushima, Japan, many Japanese felt that Tepco failed to disclose information and that the national media and government were not trustworthy either. Eighty-one percent said they did not trust government information on the crisis at the Fukushima nuclear plant (Fuji Television Network, 30 May 2011). These numbers underscore the firmly established opinion of many Japanese and other Asians that authorities and major companies don't communicate truthfully.

For retailers, the most important sentence of this book is perhaps this: **Customers in Asia do not trust easily.**

In the West if you ask shoppers which communication channels they trust the most, the customers will think of brands and of their media exposure, they may answer direct marketing, TV commercials, or internet, and some perhaps, will say word of mouth. In Asia, such as in a traditional city like Hefei in China, 300 kilometers west of Shanghai you will have nearly half of the respondents (47 percent) answering "word of mouth." This is more than TV, newspapers, and magazines together.

If you ask about the most trusted communication channel for home interior products, a category for which purchase decisions are not casual but essentially rational, word of mouth will also be number one (for about 55 percent in a place like Shanghai and more than 60 percent in less developed cities). Respondents feel that unlike other channels, personal advice through word of mouth doesn't involve a hidden motive and that it's only about sharing genuine information.

Seeing-is-believing relates directly to the notion of lack of trust. If customers don't spontaneously believe what a retail chain or a brand tells them, and if by culture they are not encouraged to express conflict or even suspicion, it is only normal that they will react by checking for themselves, visually, whatever they can verify. And if Asian customers feel they are not very knowledgeable about the quality of a product, they will rely on the only variables that show no uncertainty—the ones that can be measured and quantified.

## Retail density

In one or two generation's time, the behavior of customers in Asia may change because the demographics and physical conditions will evolve. In any given catchment area, chances are that new stores will open, whether there already is one or more outlets of the same concept and format. This will happen because retailers in Asia want to grow, and the increase of sales is generated more by expansion than by same-store growth. In cities where local governments are laid back, retailers will expand quite easily; in cities where authorities establish rules to protect the existing traditional stores, retailer will adapt but they will still expand. For instance a big box retailer may develop smaller outlets to comply with regulations, or a convenience store chain will open with a restaurant license instead of a retail license. In this case it will sell hot dogs and slurpees that customers pour from dispensing machines in addition to the usual groceries found at convenience stores.

In the emerging markets in particular, as satellite towns are built around the mega cities and as chains aim to expand into those intermediate cities, there will be a large number of medium-size stores in the new towns.

In parallel, if the price of gasoline increases significantly in the future, the effect may be that customers in Asia will tend to shop more in proximity to their homes in order to save money on transportation.

All this will trend toward a high density of medium-size outlets and each store will therefore have a smaller geographic catchment than average. As a consequence, retailers will have to focus on their primary and secondary zones.

For instance, a "small" category killer for DIY or home furnishings will cater to the needs of residents in proximity and provide mid-tier products for apartment residents or more upscale offerings for home owners, but not both. It will depend on the types of housing and the demographics of the proximity zones. A compact hypermarket or department store will also need to specialize according to local needs as opposed to aiming for a large catchment area and being all things to all people.

Hence the product range may have to be less wide but deep as the customers will still expect new arrivals and up-to-date merchandise within this focused assortment. Retailers will need to look at the primary zone and secondary zone and evaluate, for instance, whether the residents there are relatively older people or young families, and pay attention to the ratio of teenagers. If compact outlets offer a relatively wide selection but it is not deep enough, they will run the risk of failure. Conversely if retailers segment with a deep range and a less wide assortment, Asian customers will adjust their habits accordingly and may shop those medium-size stores offering a segmented assortment in their vicinity and in return, visit the 'big box' outlets less often than they used to.

In emerging countries we may experience a slightly different trend. As vehicle ownership rises, retail operators will want to saturate the markets with stores and shopping malls, and customers will be willing to visit those. Depending on how local authorities keep this under control, initiatives to open multiple stores may or may not succeed. For instance, if lots of commercial and office buildings are constructed and the government at the city level doesn't control the real estate market, there is a risk that nobody will build enough parking lots in the towns of these emerging markets and that public transport will not be a priority. In such cases, traffic will be and will remain congested. If there are more cars in town, as well as more reasons to drive to shop or to work, but no parking places and not too much public transport, traffic will not be fluid. Is it possible that towns and cities will develop in a chaotic way in the developing economies of the Far East? There are many reasons to think the answer in yes.

In both developed and developing markets, the general implication on the product range also means retailers will have to be selective when hiring merchandise buyers on behalf of the store chain. The buyer's mission will not be a routine job. i.e. negotiating as usual with producers and brand owners a certain price for a certain quantity of goods. Merchandise buyers will need to have a feel of what is pertinent on each small catchment area. If they work for a food retailer, they will need to sense whether the compact store should carry, for example, health drinks with birds nest flavor, or not. And whether imported foods are relevant; if so, which types. If they work for a furniture store chain, they'll need to discern whether a design for a table or a chair meets the likes of the people who live in the proximity zones, as opposed to a more neutral look that aims for a general public that is not differentiated.

In terms of services, customers in the near future will expect installment payment when they purchase high ticket items as opposed to the traditional habit of paying cash in some countries. They will also like entertainment at shopping destinations, either in the form of food and beverage outlets in a shopping mall, or some marketing event, or the presence of a cinema or other source of leisure. As far as staff members are concerned, we think the customers will gradually become slightly more demanding. In retail chains where shoppers expect friendliness the expectation will remain, and in chains where expertise is required, the need will potentially become more decisive.

## Electronic commerce and new concepts

The key issue as retailers continue to expand in Asia and as the density of stores increases, is the smaller geographic catchment, and the point will be to adjust the offer to residents that live in proximity.

While they reduce the format of their stores, retailers in Asia will also explore new concepts, including online shopping. Click-and-mortar also known as bricks-and-clicks is often cited as the business model of the future for retailers. If the challenge for stores based on "mortar" is to adapt their offers to local targets, for "click," e-commerce is likely to grow in Asia only for non-food items. Online shopping will probably thrive for some categories, especially in developed Asian markets but e-commerce for food will not do well because of the logistics (it is and will remain costly to deliver a few grocery items to someone's home) and because Asian people will still want to pick for themselves produce with bright colors, and to select processed foods while making sure the packaging is not damaged and the expiry date is still far away.

Beyond e-commerce itself, and as internet access expands in Asia, communication through social networks will be part of the shopper's life and part of the communication mix by retailers as well. Word of mouth will still exist but will spread online faster than it does with physical inter-actions. If retailers find ways to convey tailor-made messages through social media, a time will come when Asian customers won't be able to differentiate between genuine word of mouth and PR on the internet. Their lack of trust may then be reinforced.

Other than internet, retailers in Asia will also explore new concepts, such as hybrid types of outlets. An example would be convenience stores that are also fast food restaurants with on-premise consumption as mentioned above. Another example might be a combination of a modern trade food retailer aimed at individuals, and a cash-and-carry format, aimed at professionals.

Perhaps we should explain the difference between cash-and-carry such as Makro versus the warehouse concept like Costco, or Sam's Club. Cash-and-carry is normally used by small family-run grocery stores or hotels, restaurants and caterers (Horeca) to buy big packs and resell to the end consumers. But in several Southeast Asian countries hypermarket operators want to sell to both targets and to offer both the individual sizes (a six-pack of cans of soda, for instance) and big packs (a couple of cartons of 48 cans each). One offer targets individual households, the other is for professional retailers or for Horeca.

In the Indonesian market, LotteMart intends to develop two formats side by side, a hypermarket and a cash-and-carry store in the same commercial building. In Thailand some hypermarkets dedicate about one fifth of the store to professionals. Other retailers will want to aim for both targets more or less at parity in one stand-alone outlet. The challenge is to ensure that individual customers feel at ease in a store that looks a little bit like a cash-and-carry and for the Horeca operators to find all they want in a store that is not fully dedicated to professionals.

In other words, in the next years and decades retailers will continue to explore and test new concepts.

In any case, the respective challenges for the Asian retailers will be to reinforce penetration rates, average tickets, and frequencies of shopping depending on new customer habits.

# 11

# The Growing Asian Middle Class Presents New Challenges

HISTORICALLY, Asians have been savers because until the twentieth century they mostly experienced hardships, with a low standard of living and not much social safety net. They had to protect their families and themselves independently. However, today, even in emerging economies, a majority of residents have an income with some discretionary power, and they enjoy purchasing goods. Household incomes may not increase consistently in the region for the next one or two generations, but people may nevertheless develop new behaviors as far as shopping and spending are concerned.

For instance, shopping and eating lunch out with the family will continue to be major activities on the weekends, but the new trend is that middle class consumers will become more discriminating buyers. Stores and restaurants will need to adapt and segment their offerings, either by upgrading overall or by providing a deep selection. It goes without saying that for the upper classes in Asia there will be a growing demand for luxury items because foreign luxury brands are safe. Unlike local products, they are considered very high quality without question.

However, all this concerns behaviors due mostly to demographics and to physical conditions, as mentioned in earlier chapters. On the other hand, attitudes will not change drastically. Retailers will still have to attract the customers and make them loyal. Retail brands in the Far East will have to find merchandise that does not need to be perfect in every way, but that has something new and that shows movement and impetus, because that's what Asian shoppers will continue to want. A product with a nice price is always good, but a novelty or a new promotion that triggers interest can be better.

Permanent price and promotions do not always make customers loyal, but service from staff might. As income and education levels grow, Asian customers will appreciate services that make shopping easier, avoid a waste of time, offer reassurance about product safety, and provide a harmonious atmosphere in the store. In particular store managers must invest in a minimum level of training for employees, which should include product knowledge when expertise is relevant, but also about teaching friendliness and that employees are there to facilitate the shopping experience. Stores in Asia will need to do at least two things: first, establish some 'momentum' about the merchandise offer by providing new products and more depth than in the past, and second, improve goodwill towards their customers. This is not just a nice thing to do. It relates to the customers' need for seeing and to the important cultural need for harmony.

The retailers that will win the battle in the coming decades in Asia are the ones that stay focused on their customers because

- They have the corporate cultures to genuinely care about their shoppers,
- As companies, they focus on loyalty-building, or
- They are already used to working in a relatively small geographic catchment area.

In any case, they will be successful if they do not forget to be customer-friendly people, not just bottom-line people.

We hope this book will assist retailers, as well as brand owners, in their quest to understand, to meet the needs and wants, and ultimately to earn the trust of shoppers in Asia.

# Bibliography

Coates, Austin, *Myself A Mandarin: Memoirs of a Special Magistrate*, Heinemann Educational Books, 1978.

Confucius, *Analects*, (various publishers).

Hall, Edward T., Beyond Culture, New York: Anchor Books, 1976.

Humby, Clive, Terry Hunt, and Tim Phillips, *Scoring Points: How Tesco Continues to Win Customer Loyalty*, London: Kogan Page, 2008.

Levi-Strauss, Claude, *The Savage Mind*, Chicago: University of Chicago Press, 1968.

Osborne, Milton E., "History and Kinship in Contemporary Cambodia," 1966.

Plato, *The Republic*, (various publishers).

Reichheld, Frederick, *The Ultimate Question: Driving Good Profits and True Growth*, Cambridge, MA: Harvard Business Press, 2006.

Reilly, William, *The Law of Retail Gravitation*, Pilsbury Publishers, 1972.

Spector, Robert, *Category Killers: The Retail Revolution and Its Impact on Consumer Culture*, Cambridge, MA: Harvard Business Press, 2005.

# Index

# About the author

LAURENT SAUSSET is a consultant with 25 years marketing experience in Asia.

Born in France in 1959, he has also lived in Canada and Africa. After earning a graduate business degree in France, he began his career in 1985 in Tokyo with Nichifutsu Boeki, importing and selling European consumer products and technical goods in Japan. He then joined the Remy Martin group and was in charge of sales and marketing in Asia from 1989 to 1995, while the brand progressed in volume from number three in the region to number one. In 1995 Laurent was hired by the headquarters of The Walt Disney Company as Director, Corporate Brand Management for Asia. In this capacity, based in Hong Kong, he oversaw the Disney brand exposure including Walt Disney Pictures, Licensed Products, The Disney Store and Theme Parks for Greater China, India and Southeast Asia. The Disney brand enjoyed an increasingly high overall regard in those countries. In 1999 Laurent joined a European marketing consultancy, S.A.D.A. as Managing Director of its subsidiary in Taipei and developed sales in Taiwan and the rest of the Asia-Pacific, focusing its expertise on retail marketing.

Laurent started his own boutique consultancy, DistriSurvey Ltd. in early 2004, specializing in shopping behavior and attitudes in the Far East markets. Over the years he has advised major Western retail chains in Asia such as Walmart, Carrefour, Casino Group, RtMart, Kingfisher

B&Q, Leroy Merlin, Office Depot, Toys'R'Us, as well as Asian retailers including Wellcome, Tops, Giant, Hymal, Lotte, Jusco, Robinson, Central and Far Eastern department stores.

Occasionally Laurent writes articles for Chinese retail magazines and is also a speaker about Asian customers shopping behavior and retail sales forecasting methods in cities as various as Bangkok, Taipei, and Seoul.

Laurent has lived in Japan, Hong Kong, Taiwan and currently resides in Thailand with his wife Siriwan. He spends 90 percent of his time in the Asian markets.

# About DistriSurvey Ltd

DISTRISURVEY LTD was established in Asia in 2004, stemming from a strategic observation: there was no marketing consultancy in the Far East that truly specialized in retail marketing.

Several market research companies and marketing gurus in the region addressed retail in terms of trends or volumes of sales, or would analyze end consumer habits such as general attitudes or product usage. However, they did not concentrate on what happens in a store; why Asian people shop the way they do; why a store generates a certain level of sales and transactions.

DistriSurvey focuses on knowing the shopper, and aims to pinpoint what the shopper knows and experiences in a retail environment.

With analysts and managers in China, Taiwan, and Thailand, and a representative office in Hong Kong, DistriSurvey also has appointed research partners in the other main markets of Asia: Japan, Korea, Vietnam, Cambodia, Malaysia, Singapore, and Indonesia. All the teams have been working with the same questionnaires, same interview approaches, and same overall methodologies.

"Distri" as the clients call DistriSurvey Ltd works on improving the performance of stores, once they are open. The goal can be to capture more customers, or to encourage them to visit more frequently, or to increase their spending when they shop. Methods used include accompanied shopping, exit surveys, one-on-one in-home interviews, focus group discussions, and mystery shopping. Statistic treatments to identify correlations and to determine what builds customer loyalty act as tools to discern what is critical for retailers vs. what is secondary.

DistriSurvey also helps retailers with market-entry, and helps answer strategic questions such as: "Is there a potential for our chain in this country?" "How many stores can we open in this province?" and "What specific needs and wants are essential?" DistriSurvey is virtually the only independent firm in Asia that is also capable of forecasting sales for a store project. Given specific data—location, store format, net sales area, parking lot, co-anchors, etc.—DistriSurvey provides answers to the critical question, "What sales turnover can we expect to achieve?"